# THE LIFE STORY OF TANNEKEN FROS

## FOLLOWING JESUS

COME
WHAT
MAY

By Tanneken Fros with Maria Stuart

## TCF Mercy

TCF Mercy Publishing
Goshen, Indiana

© TCF Mercy Publishing 2016

Printed in the United States of America

ISBN-13: 978-0692651520
ISBN-10: 0692651527

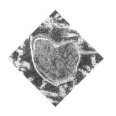

# Contents

# Introduction

*Childhood scenes rushed back at me out of the night,
strangely close and urgent. Today I know such memories
are the key not to the past, but to the future. I know that
the experiences of our lives, when we let God use them,
become the mysterious and perfect preparation
for the work He will give us to do.*
Corrie Ten Boom, "The Hiding Place"[1]

It was the spring of 2010 in Beira, Mozambique, the country's second largest city. The bus stop outside the hospital was always busy. People congregated in wait for the elusive *chapa* minibus that would take them out of the city. Street sellers hawking cheap doughnuts and phone credit stood in the way of any likely customer. When the *chapa* finally arrived, people crammed through the sliding door trying to get a seat, over 20 crowding into a bus licensed for 15. Some missed out and grumbled. Injured and disabled people were given the best seat. The doormen of buses on less popular routes shouted their destination; drivers revved their engines pretending to leave and then stayed another 10 minutes trying to fill the seats.

My children and I regularly picked our way through this melee, trying not to trip on the crumbling pavements, sometimes to catch a bus, most times to go to the beach. But today was different. The crowds were enormous, hundreds of people sat all over the pavements, but they were not going anywhere. Nor were they trying to catch a bus—they were reading.

Tanneken was there with a group from her church. They had just been into the hospital for their weekly visit to pray for patients. Now they were handing out booklets, small tracts explaining the gospel of Christ. Hundreds of people had stopped in the midst of their day's business and journeys to sit and read the message they contained.

When we walked back later on, not a booklet was to be seen thrown away as rubbish.

But Tanneken could not stay long. Now she was off to the school for blind and visually impaired children to pick up students, some of them orphans, for their weekend stay at her home. This is Tanneken, in her sixties, doing all she can, whenever she can, wherever she can, for Jesus and for His people. She's probably late, she's probably forgotten something, and yet she never fails to be open to be used by God.

During our year living in Mozambique, my family was privileged to get to know Tanneken and to experience her love and support. We spent a precious Easter weekend in her home, shared with orphans and a widow out in the more rural town of Dondo. Our children played with her children, drew water from the well, and watched TV. We got to know and love Lenora, a young woman from the Bruderhof, the community in which Tanneken had grown up.

Before dawn on Saturday, we joined Tanneken and her church on an hour's walk through the rice fields, chatting and singing worship songs, to a pond where we watched 29 people being baptized – adults, young people, one old man, and our English friend Jo. Tanneken, with her church elders, braved murky water where snakes lurk without fear or concern to baptize these new believers. Elders preached, and Tanneken translated and prayed for many of those baptized, very much part of this Mozambican church, accepted by all, and supportive of all, not given any special treatment as many of us foreigners often are.

When Tanneken begins to open up her life to you, your mind fills with questions, wanting to know more. I asked her if she had ever thought of writing down her story. "Yes, it's been prophesied!" was her reply. So, in a five-minute conversation, this book was begun. I was soon handed many old cassette tapes of Tanneken telling her story while she sat on the beach with the waves and the wind competing with her words.

Tanneken's story is not the story of one woman alone. Throughout her life, God has given her significant people who have supported her, prayed for her, brought her the message of salvation in Jesus, taught her and mentored her, gone behind her and sorted out administrative and technical problems, found her glasses for her, and gone back for her forgotten keys. She has stood behind others, supporting them as they developed significant ministries both in Israel and in Mozambique. Her home church has allowed her mission to grow and change, and has supported her every step of the way. She has friends who have been praying for her for over 30 years, some of whom we will hear from in the coming chapters. If you are one of those people, Tanneken knows she could not have followed her calling without you. You have been part of the increase of the Kingdom of Heaven on earth that Tanneken has been privileged to witness.

For the most part, Tanneken tells her own story in this book. Some names have been changed to protect their privacy. Often at the end of chapters, other voices appear. Her brother Melchior fills us in on Christmastime in Paraguay. Her friends, Pat and Kay, talk of the quiet, withdrawn girl they first met, and the change they saw as she found personal faith in Jesus. Joana, a young blind Mozambican girl who has lived with Tanneken on school holidays for over eight years, tells us her story. The life story of Pastor Rego, with whom Tanneken has worked alongside for many years, is told in an appendix.

One friend sees Tanneken as "uniquely prepared for her current ministry." Perhaps in this, she is like the apostle Paul, whose background as a Pharisee and a Roman citizen by birth, perfectly prepared him for taking the gospel to the Gentiles and Jews scattered throughout the Roman Empire. Life has taken Tanneken from birth in rural Paraguay in South America to Europe and America. In her forties, she entered Christian service in Israel, and then, past her fiftieth birthday, into mission in Mozambique. This is her story of struggle, joyful sacrifice, and obedience to the call of Jesus.

Maria Stuart

*2010: The MOP Church is returning from a baptism done in a small river in the rice fields of Dondo. Everyone is rejoicing, singing and waving palm branches.*

# Named and Loved

*I will praise You, for I am fearfully and wonderfully made.*
Psalm 139:14a

My precious Mama and Papa waited for me. They so hoped that I would be born on Christmas, but I chose a few days after. I was born on December 28, 1945. I was told that the night I was born a bright shooting star fell from the sky. I do not interpret this as some people interpret the stars, but I do know that God speaks through His creation. I believe God knew me even before I was born. Psalm 139:13-16 speaks so beautifully of this:

> For You formed my inward parts; You covered me in my mother's womb. I will praise You, for I am fearfully and wonderfully made; marvelous are Your works, and that my soul knows very well. My frame was not hidden from You, When I was made in secret, and skillfully wrought in the lowest parts of the earth. Your eyes saw my substance, being yet unformed. And in Your book they all were written, the days fashioned for me, when as yet there were none of them.

Mama and Papa had searched for many a name. Because they were Anabaptists, they were very familiar with a book called *The Martyr's Mirror*. This book is about two and a half inches thick and is filled with incredible testimonies of Christians who suffered and were martyred for their faith in Jesus Christ in the 16th and 17th centuries. They were burned at the stake and drowned in rivers for their unwavering stand against false teachings within the church of that day.

Mama and Papa were moved by the testimony of a little child called Tanneken, orphaned when her parents were martyred. Because of the letter that was left behind by her mother, Soetken Van den Route, I am sure God's hand was on this child. Little Tanneken's father had already been burned at the stake, and Soetken was about to face the same death. She wrote a farewell letter to her children. It was this letter of courage, faith, and wise Christian counsel that caused my parents to choose Tanneken as my name:

A TESTAMENT OF SOETGEN VAN DEN ROUTE, WHICH SHE LEFT HER CHILDREN, DAVID, BETGEN AND TANNEKEN, FOR A MEMORIAL, AND FOR THE BEST, AND WHICH SHE CONFIRMED WITH HER DEATH, AT GHENT, FLANDERS

*In the name of the Lord:*

*Grace, peace and mercy from God the Father and the Lord Jesus Christ, this I wish you, my dear little children, David, Betgen, and Tanneken, for an affectionate greeting, written by your mother in bonds, for a memorial to you of the truth, as I hope to testify by word and with my death, by the help of the Most High, for an example unto you. May the wisdom of the Holy Ghost instruct and strengthen you therein, that you may be brought up in the ways of the Lord. Amen.*

*Further my dear children, since it pleases the Lord to take me out of this world, I will leave you a memorial, not of silver or gold; for such jewels are perishable: but I should like to write a jewel into your heart, if it were possible, which is the word of truth, in which I want to instruct you a little for the best with the Word of the Lord, according to the little gift I have received from Him and according to my simplicity.*

*...Further, my dear children, Betgen and Tanneken, my beloved lambs, I admonish you in all these same things, as that you obey the commandments of the Lord, and also obey your uncle and aunt, and your elders, and all who instruct you in virtue. To those whose bread you eat, you must be subject in all that is not contrary to God. Always diligently admonish yourselves to do your work, and you will be loved wherever you live. Be not quarrelsome, or loquacious, or light minded, or proud, or surly of speech, but kind, honorable and quiet, as behooves young girls. Pray the Lord for wisdom, and it shall be given you. Diligently learn to read and write, and take delight therein, and you will become wise. Take pleasure and engage in psalms, hymns and spiritual songs. Seek for the only joy. Learn to please the Lord from your youth, as did the holy women and virgins, as Judith.*

*... O my dear lambs, see that you do not spend your youth in vanity, or pride, or drinking, or gluttony, but in sobriety and humility in the*

*fear of God, and diligence in every good work, that you may be clothed with the adornment of the saints, so that God may make you worthy through His grace, to enter in to the marriage of the Lamb, and that we may see you there with joy. Your father and I, and many others, have shown you the way. Take an example from the prophets and apostles, yea, Christ Himself, who all went this way; and where the head has gone before, there the members must certainly follow.*

*...Herewith I bid you adieu, my dear child Betgen; adieu, my dear children David and Tanneken; adieu...*

*Written by me Soetgen van den Houte, your mother in bonds; written in haste (while trembling with cold), out of love for you all. Amen.*

(Written on November 27, 1560)[1]

What courage, what faith these parents had. I pray that like my parents that named me after her, I too will always remain faithful to

follow Jesus. He is my Shepherd; He is my Lord; He is my all in all; He is the One who carries me.

Since I was born at Christmas, my parents also associated my name with the lovely fir trees used at Christmas (*tannenbaum* in German) to decorate the homes, lit with candles reminding us that Jesus is the Light of the world. My parents would often say, "Here comes our little Tannenbaum." And so I came into the world with the love of my parents and the love of the Lord.

*My family, October 1947—Left to right, front row: Hänsel (Hans), Jan Peter (died at age eight of rheumatic fever of the heart); middle row: Mechthild, Mama (Susi) holding baby Susi-Lucia, Irene; back row: Papa holding me (two years old)*

# Faithful Parents

*Now all who believed were together, and had all things
in common, and sold their possessions and goods, and
divided them among all, as anyone had need.*
Acts 2:44-45

My full name is Tanneken Cornelia Fros. I am of European descent.
My father, Jan, was Dutch and was born in Leiden in the Netherlands.
My mother, Susi, was German, born in the area of Hamburg, in the
Schleswig-Holstein district. My parents were very faithful devout
Christians. Before they met, both joined a Christian community
called the Bruderhof.

This community found much affinity with an older Anabaptist group,
the Hutterites, who had seen centuries of persecution in Europe. They
were particularly disliked because of their practice of the "common
purse" and their pacifist stance as demonstrated when they refused
to pay war taxes. At that time, the Hutterites lived mainly in Canada,
but the Bruderhof formally united with them in 1930.

These Anabaptist Christians, to the best of their understanding,
wanted to live a fuller Christian life, as taught by Jesus in the Sermon on
the Mount. They were in part also disillusioned with the state church
and church life at large, and they sincerely sought to live a Christian
community life, where everything was shared in common. No one
called anything his own, and everyone shared with his neighbor.

My mother joined the Bruderhof in 1933 while studying philosophy
and theology at Tübingen University in southern Germany. During
the last semester of her studies, some Bruderhof brethren came to
the university to share about their communal life style. Mother and
her best friend Edith were convinced to join the community, so they
left their studies at Tübingen without notifying their parents. When
mother's parents found out that she had left her studies to join the

Bruderhof, they sent police to take her out of the community and return her to the university to finish her studies. But this did not work; Mother and Edith stayed, living in an old farmhouse near Fulda in the Rhön Mountains in Germany.

It was during this time, in the early 1930s, when Hitler rose to power. The Bruderhof members were determined that they wanted to follow Jesus unconditionally. When Hitler came to power, he demanded that all people had to serve him and hail him and one another with the salute "Heil Hitler." In German, the word *heil* means salvation. Jesus' name in German is *Heiland* and Jesus *der Heiland*, Jesus the Savior. From this, one can see that Hitler put himself equal to Christ, at least for the Germans. Each of us has to make a decision in life, who we will serve. At that time, the members of the Bruderhof made the choice not to "Heil Hitler." While they did not openly oppose the Nazi regime, this small act of not using the Nazi salute was a dangerous act of defiance.

The community's daily struggles to stand up under the Nazi regime are well recorded.[1] Not saying "Heil Hitler" in shops was defiance enough but they did more and boldly proclaimed their position in official letters. Though they promised to pray for Hitler, they also declared that the word "heil" belonged for Christ alone.[2] Their first real battle came in the election of November 12, 1933. Unable to support the National Socialist Party or any of its supporters—the only choices on the ballot—the community made the decision to form a joint statement explaining their Christian position, which they attached to their individual ballots, putting their loyalty to Christ as their highest calling above their commitment to Germany and its leaders. In this way they joined 3.3 million other Germans in protesting this unfair election, but the National Socialist Party still received 92.2% of the nation's votes.

May 1952: My grandparents, Opa Geret and Oma Cornelia Fros, at home in Loma Hoby, Paraguay at the Bruderhof Community

Just four days later, their community was raided by the regime. It is written that 140-160 uniformed and armed men carried out this raid. Each member was interrogated—including my dear mother.[3] This raid soon led to the closing of their school, the sending away of foster children, the ban on outside visitors, and an attempt to reclaim some of their farmland—all steps that damaged the financial footing of the community, preventing them from carrying out their mission of loving others through community life. In the next few years many of the community moved to Liechtenstein (just west of Austria) and later to England to avoid state schools and conscription.

Finally, on April 14, 1937, the Nazi Police surrounded and entered the Rhön Bruderhof, as it was then called. Community members were given 48 hours to leave, but its three elders were arrested. The community was able to flee the country together on the evening of April 16, and the elders were released some weeks later and helped to flee the country. One Bruderhof group fled via Holland and stayed there two months.

My father, Jan, together with his parents, Gerrit and Cornelia Fros, met the Bruderhof at this time. They, too, were disillusioned with the state church and sought a fuller expression of the Christian walk. My father heard of this Anabaptist community that had come to Holland and spent much time with them. But all too soon, the whole community had to move, this time to England. My father decided to join them. As my father made his decision to live in Christian community, he took the few coins he had out of his pocket, laid them on the table, and said, "I am with you for the rest of my life." My grandparents and one of my father's brothers, Herman, joined the community soon after.

Papa met my dear Mama in England. They didn't *fall* in love with each other; they *grew* in love for each other. Mama was 28 years old and thought, "I will never marry. I am too old already." Papa was the milkman. After milking the cows, he would bring the barrel of milk to the community. One day, Mama was on the top floor in her room standing at a window, and Mama waved at Papa. Papa waved back and then spilt all the milk! They got married a few months later and had their first child, Irene, whilst still in England.

These one or two years in England came to an abrupt halt as the Second World War broke out in 1939. At first most German nationals were allowed to remain at liberty in the United Kingdom, unless they were considered a threat. However, as time went on, suspicion and internment of German civilians increased. Men were sent to separate camps from their families,[4] so the Bruderhof fled again. They tried to go to America or Canada, but they were not allowed in. The only country that welcomed them was Paraguay in central South America.

In 1940—an incredibly dangerous time to be undertaking such a journey—the first group left England by ship across the Atlantic. My parents and little Irene, along with many other community members, traveled on the Blue Star Line ship, *The Andalucia Star*, in November 1940.[5] At night on the deep seas, everything had to be dark, so the ship would not be torpedoed. Miraculously, it didn't sink at this time; however in October 1942 on its return journey from Buenos Aires, the ship was torpedoed off the coast of West Africa and foundered. Its sister ship, *The Almeda Star*, which left England just two months after my parents' ship, was also torpedoed and sunk off the coast of Scotland losing all 360 people on board.[6] Three weeks later, a further 159 Bruderhof members—including my grandparents, Gerrit and Cornelia—crossed the Atlantic on the *Avila Star*[7] and made the journey safely. As far as I know, no community members were lost on this treacherous crossing.

When they arrived in Paraguay, they came first to the Chaco. This desert land, a very far stretching piece of land in the northwest of Paraguay, was just brush, very thorny, and where little of anything grew. There they met the Mennonites, who had fled the First World War and settled in the Chaco. Mennonites are Christians who show much compassion and mercy; they help all over the world to this day.[8] I well remember my mother and father telling me, with much appreciation, "If it had not been for these Mennonites, we would not have survived."

During this traumatic transition in life, my mother was heavily pregnant with my oldest brother, Jan Peter. For days they traveled by riverboat and then carts pulled by a horse or an ox to the Chaco. There were no roads, just dirt tracks with deep holes and mud—a very difficult situation. You can imagine what Mama and two other women who were in the same situation had to suffer through, as they were getting ready to give birth. They were in a very hot sub-tropical climate and had no houses that afforded the normal comforts available for such a delicate time. But the Mennonites took them in. To this day, we are thankful as a family for the help they offered us at this time. Jan Peter was born on January 4, 1941, just two days after they had arrived in the Chaco.[9]

It was after this that the Bruderhof community moved onto another portion of Paraguay, northeast of Asunción, to a strip of land called

Primavera, which in Spanish means "spring." It was not a village, just jungle with wide prairie land, uninhabited, very hot, many mosquitoes, crocodiles, and all sorts of wild animals including wild cats. It was difficult, although strikingly beautiful, and a slightly easier climate for European refugees than the Chaco. They had nothing, absolutely nothing. But I know the protecting hand of God was over their lives, as I know the protecting hand of God has been over my life until this day. Life had started for the Bruderhof in Paraguay.

# Life in Paraguay

*Müde bin ich, geh' zur Ruh', Schließe beide Äuglein zu;*
*Vater, laß die Augen dein Über meinem Bette sein!*

*I am tired and I will go to rest, closing my eyes.*
*Father, let your eyes watch over me.*[1]

Evening prayer sung by Tanneken's Mama

My parents were good parents. I cannot remember one fight. I'm sure Mama and Papa had their arguments, but if they did, they must have done it on the side, not in front of us. I am thankful for the values they raised us with. They were industrious people. My father was an assistant pharmacist in the hospital that we had later in the Paraguayan community. He was also a biology teacher in our school; his love for flowers and all God's creation was evident in his classes and was passed down to several of us children. To this day, some of his students speak very dearly of him.

However, for most of my childhood, Papa worked as a storekeeper, distributing the food for the community. As children who loved an extra treat, we would pass by the storeroom, knowing that Papa was there. He often gave us a banana, an egg, or a little cookie to nibble on. We had so little of this, so it was always a special treat.

Papa was also gifted in music. He had the tenor voice of an angel. When Papa sang, I would think of the archangel Gabriel. I was especially moved when he sang Handel's *Messiah*, that God-given, Holy Spirit-inspired, great work celebrating Jesus. He also played the violin and loved to compose music. We were privileged to sing a beautiful cantata he wrote about creation. My whole family loved music, so I grew up loving to sing. Papa told me that every night when I was around two years old, I said, "No Papa, before we sleep, let's dance!"

So he would dance with me every night to the children's song, "Tanz, tanz, Quieselchen."

My mother was a woman of determination, which I believe is one of the virtues I inherited from her. She was a very good school teacher and my teacher as well. Being strict, she got things done, for which I am glad. Mama played the piano and had a beautiful soprano voice. Even though the word of God was not spoken much in the family, every night my mother would sing an evening prayer at our bedside. That was the only prayer I heard my mother say in my childhood. I still remember the words to one of the verses: "If I have done anything wrong today, dear God, do not hold that against me. Your grace and the blood of Jesus will take away all our failings."[2] This

My third year birthday party in the Loma Hoby Bruderhof community. My mother is the teacher. I am facing the camera.

is an especially dear verse for me, because I sang it with my mother on my final visit with her when she was 91 years old!

There were seven children in our family, and we were a happy family. Irene was born in England. She played the violin and became a music teacher after studying in the neighboring country of Uruguay. She was very close to me and looked after me, and I looked up to her.

A tropical Christmas in Paraguay, 1951. At age six I created this Christmas picture of an Angel flying with a candle.

My brother, Jan Peter, was born in the Chaco. We lost him at eight years of age with rheumatic fever of the heart. Today, this disease has a very successful cure. We were told he was a very gentle boy, who loved animals and the local Paraguayans. He was very compassionate. One day he saw

Another piece of art I created in 1951 depicts Resurrection Day with an Angel sitting on Jesus' tomb.

that one of the Paraguayans who worked with us had no bed. So he went home and said to my mother and father, "He needs a bed. We must give him a bed; we must give him a mattress." I'm sure those pleas worked on my parents' hearts to produce the needed mattress and bed. Jan Peter also had a playful side. Even though he had to have many injections and was very weak at the end, he would play tricks on the nurse. After she had finished the injections, he would fill the syringe with water and squirt it at her, or he would hide from her. He always found some way to play.

After Jan Peter came Hänsel, or Hans, who loved God's creation, animals and nature alike. Like the rest of the family, he loved music and played the guitar. I still enjoy hearing his beautiful tenor voice, which he only uses to sing about Jesus. When I hear him sing, I hear my father sing. Then came Mechthild, my dear sister with a gift of laughter. She played the guitar and the recorder beautifully.

I was the fifth in the Fros family. I played the violin, the guitar, and the recorder. I loved to sing to my Jesus and still do. There's nothing more beautiful to do than to sing to my Jesus, the lover of my soul. I love You, my Jesus! May my life and all our lives be a love song to You. After me came Susi-Lucia, who had a quiet nature and played the flute and recorder. The last one in the Fros family was my youngest brother Melchior. Because I always looked after him in our younger years, we had a special bond. He sang many beautiful German folk songs with his guitar.

I'm very thankful for the courage and faithfulness to Jesus that my parents demonstrated, not just in fleeing Nazi Germany, but also in settling in Paraguay and raising such a large family in difficult, pioneer-like circumstances. But their love reached far beyond their own family. Because they were part of a Christian community where everybody shared everything in common, they had a heart for the poor, the needy, and the unwanted. Many of the children had serious conditions such as eye diseases and malaria. They were Europeans who were not used to sub-tropical temperatures and high humidity, so they also suffered from the heat.

Our home in Loma Hoby, one of the three communities built by the Bruderhof at Primavera, was on an open plain, but very close to the jungle. There were ants, snakes, and armadillos, as well as crocodiles in the rivers. I remember when we came home from an evening event to find our house full of ants. These ants went on migrations, passing through the whole village. If you didn't disturb them it was okay, but if you did, you'd better watch out! They would go over anything in their way. The only one left at home that evening was Melchior, who we found covered in ants—in his hair, over his face, everywhere! Though we ran in to get him and rid him of all the ants, he was badly stung.

The community's homes were very simple, mainly wood. Each family had two or three bedrooms, but the bathrooms were outside of the house. You had to go to the common place to take a bath or use the bathroom, which was perhaps a two or even ten minute walk from your house. The outhouses were just a deep hole in the ground. A floor covered the ground, and a wooden seat covered the hole. But they would get rickety, and we children were petrified that we would fall into the holes! Once a child did fall in but was rescued. At night, we were too afraid to go, so I think every family had their own bucket in the house for the night!

Lightning storms are very strong in the tropics. I remember during one very severe thunderstorm, the whole family was huddled in the house. There was no glass in the window frames, just an open window and a wooden shutter. We had not closed our shutters yet, when suddenly this fireball around five inches in diameter flew through the house past our heads, right through the living room from one window to the other, and out, hitting a papaya tree. When we went out outside after the storm, it was just ashes inside the trunk. Though I do not remember much spiritual talk or prayers about such natural events, I know that I did not grow up in fear. We felt quite safe in our Christian community environment.

Every family was fully integrated into the community life. A newborn stayed with the mother at home for six weeks. Then he went to the common baby house and spent the day there. During the day, the mother visited him there to feed him. All the children were cared for in the common houses: babies in the baby house, toddlers in the toddler house, kindergarten children in the kindergarten, and so on. Once children reached their high school years, they went on to public high school and later on to college to train for a profession.

For lunch and dinner, families all ate in the common dining room or in the children's departments. Nobody cooked at home except for breakfast of a cup of *yerba maté*, a tea brewed from a local plant. Sometimes we fried a piece of *mandioca*, commonly known as cassava, and put a little syrup on it, or a piece of bread. Lunch and evening meals were simple meals, but we never went hungry.

At the Isla Bruderhof community, 1952: My Aunt Nellie (Papa's sister) and Uncle Alan with their seven children

Life in the community had a very regular rhythm. Early in the morning, the family would breakfast together in the family home. At eight o'clock, all the children went to the common houses, and the men went to work. The women stayed home until nine o'clock to finish whatever they needed to do in the house and then reported to their allocated work departments, be it the kitchen, the laundry, the sewing room, or the school. At a quarter past twelve when the common big bell rang, all the men and women went to the common dining room to have their lunch at half past twelve. At one o'clock, there was a rest period. At two o'clock, the fathers returned to their work, but the mothers stayed home for another hour with the children. Then the mothers returned to their work departments and the children to their children's departments and school until half past five.

The children—from one-year-old toddlers to fifth grade eleven year olds—had their supper in their departments. At half past five, families were together in the home until seven. All adults, youth, and upper-school grades went to the dining room for the common evening meal. Younger children stayed at home and were guarded by what we called "the watch," someone who watched the children while the parents were eating. In the evenings, there was often a prayer meeting or a membership evening.

The whole principle of living in community and having everything in common was based on what the early Christians in Jerusalem experienced after waiting for God's promise of the outpouring of the Holy Spirit as recorded in Acts 2:42-46:

And they continued steadfastly in the apostles' doctrine and fellowship, in the breaking of bread, and in prayers. Then fear came upon every soul, and many wonders and signs were done through the apostles. Now all who believed were together, and had all things in common, and sold their possessions and goods, and divided them among all, as anyone had need. So continuing daily with one accord in the temple, and breaking bread from house to house, they ate their food with gladness and simplicity of heart...

They had a common purse, so there was no private income. In Paraguay, the work was mainly agricultural. The community had a big cowherd, pigs and chickens, and many fields; in later years, they had rice fields. They crafted beautiful wooden vases and bowls in a common workshop and sold them in Asunción, the capital. This was their main income-generating business. With this money, they bought all the medicines for the hospital, which served not only our own needs but also ministered to local Paraguayans.

When the community started planting new communities in the United States in the 1950s, they started making playthings such as wooden toys and nursery school furniture. Today, their main income, I believe, comes from making various kinds of equipment, including items for use in physical therapy with disabled people.

I remember being a very active child. I loved to hike and go on nature walks, and I was one of the strongest ones in sports, as far as the girls were concerned. The boys always chose me first when it came to Völkerball, a game a little bit like "Pig in the Middle," but done in teams. Growing up in a setting with many, many children perhaps helped prepare me for the work I have today with orphans.

In school, we had very simple facilities. We had a blackboard and a notebook, and whatever the teacher wrote on the blackboard, we copied into our

1955: I (left) am on a field trip with my fourth grade classmates to the Loma Hoby community "airport," which was just a strip of grassland.

*Family outing on the Paraguay River in 1959. I'm the one holding the pole.*

notebook. We grew up bilingually, speaking both German and English. Whatever the teacher spoke was the language of the classroom. Our school teachers were from Europe, so they were German, British, Swiss, and Dutch. One of my favorite classes was music class. At twelve years old, I started to learn the violin. Since my sister Irene had been playing the violin for some years, I was eager to learn to play as well as she did.

One of our favorite events was the annual field trip. We had no cars or bicycles; we went everywhere on foot, by horse, or in a cart pulled by oxen. It took us hours to get to a river deep in the jungle, where we stayed for two or three days. What excitement as we saw the water glistening in the sunshine! On the last stretch, we raced to see who could get there first, but everybody helped unpack the wagon. The large hut that we stayed in was very simple. Our beds were wooden planks nailed together in a row. Mosquito nets were fastened, and the kitchen was set up. We all had to help gather firewood, for everything was cooked on a campfire.

Once camp was set up, we were free to swim, go on a boat ride with a paddle boat, or hike in the jungle. We saw monkeys opening sweet, wild oranges, and it wasn't uncommon to hear a water hog snorting or see a snake curled around a branch. For play, we raced to see who could find the most parrot feathers. Night time was just as entertaining. Strange, sometimes scary sounds of night birds and hooting owls were all around us. Large camp fires lit up the darkness, as we threw lit branches into the river. One of our teachers even searched the river for the glowing eyes of crocodiles swimming in the black water!

I did well in school, although I had to work very hard for my grades. My parents and teachers told me that I always tried to make peace among the children, but I have to be honest...at home there wasn't always peace. In fact, the seven of us loved to quarrel, but that phase passed. I wish I hadn't quarreled so much in the family, but outside with the other children, in general, it was peaceful.

At thirteen, I became aware of wanting to follow Jesus. Within the community at that time the emphasis was very much on doing good works. I had yet to understand that while "faith without works is dead," works alone without faith are of no value. So at thirteen years old, I very much wanted to do well for others. I remember a couple, Maria and Adolpho, who came to live with us at Primavera. Maria had leprosy and had to live in a little cottage by herself, but we were allowed to visit her. I was part of a children's prayer group called the Sonnen Truppe, and one day I said, "Let's go and sing to Maria," so we sang Jesus songs to her. It was lovely for us to do good in this way, and for me it was the only way I knew to follow Jesus.

I'm thankful for the values we were taught. We were encouraged to do our work well and to be creative with the little that we had. We were taught not to swear and to respect God's creation and love and care for one another. I especially remember Christmas, which was a very special time for us. We were so poor, but somehow the community managed to make a few sweet cookies for us, and some of the adults made little cloth dolls or a simple wooden cart to push our dolls in. I remember my brother Jan Peter having a little wooden truck, the only toy I remember him playing with. We girls had one dress, maybe two, and we usually were barefoot, but for Christmas, they gave us wooden sandals with simple leather straps. We had so little, but we were happy and content.

Christmas was one of the times the community would have wonderful celebrations. I will never forget when, as a young boy, my brother Melchior sang the solo part as one of the three wise men in the Christmas drama of "Amahl and the Night Visitors," directed by my father. The words are so lovely:

> The child we seek does not need our gold.
> On love, on love alone, He will found His kingdom.
> His pierced hand will hold no sceptre.
> His haloed head will wear no crown;
> His life will not be built on our toil.
> Swifter than lightning, He will soon walk among us;
> He will bring us new life and receive us from death,
> And the keys to His Kingdom, belong to the poor.[3]

All in all, I had a happy childhood. But within the community, a difficult time was coming that would change our family's life forever.

# From Melchior, the youngest Fros

### Christmas in Paraguay

Kommt all herzu, ihr Engelein,
Kommt all herein,
Und helft mir wiegen das Kindelein,
Im Krippelein...

Come hither, come to me, you angels all,
Come enter this stall.
And help me cradle the Son of all,
In His crib so small...

Mainzer Cantonal, 1628, translated by Melchior Fros

It's December 24, 1955, and my family is busy decorating the family room. We make paper stars from colored and silver papers which our Grossmutter sent us from Germany. We tie colored threads to the stars. We make hand dipped candles too. Mama uses a fretsaw, and cuts delicate crib scene figures from a thin, white material. We cut angel figures from wood, paint them, and glue them to wood bases. A nail hammered through the back of each base secures the candle. Papa is busy in the community storehouse filling pillow cases with cookies, carefully measured according to family size. Each family gets a banana catch and one bottle of homemade wine. My Papa makes good wine!

Around noon, in the company of my brother and my sisters, we cross the horse pasture, the Piquette, as it is known. Bone-thin Karopeh, "our horse", grazes nearby. We pass by the I-Wäldchen, a densely wooded "island" in a sea of marshy campo grass land. We enter the forest and look for a suitable "Christmas tree." Hänsel carries a machete, and he cuts a decent branch from an Ivirapeppe.

We carry it home together, stick it in a bucket full of sand, and put it in the corner of the family room. We decorate the "tree" with paper stars and silver strands of lametta. Each strand is carefully hung on the "tree"; nothing goes to waste. Other handmade decorations are hung on the tree. Boughs are nailed above bedroom doors and over window openings, and straw stars are hung from them. We put a wooden crib scene under the tree.

Papa, my village's general store keeper, comes home and helps us put real candles on the "tree". He fills a bucket of water and places it nearby. There are no twinkling lights; no gaudy glitz. The only artificial light comes from a single 40 watt bulb, dangling from the ceiling. It goes out at 10 pm. Papa tells me to go out and play. I look for my young rooster, Zarbiets, catch him and put him under my upside-down wheelbarrow for the night. I think he'll be safe from foxes. I pretend not to look, but I see my father sawing, hammering and putting together something made from a small Seifenkiste, a soap box.

*It's 1959 and that's me with my adopted cat, Pino, by the family dwelling in the Isla Margarita Community.*

By now it's 5 pm and my sisters Tanneken and Susi walk me to the Kindergarten, way down at the other end of my village. My group has to take a siesta nap before the Christmas angels and the community fetch us, and we go to the cow stall, where we will see Joseph and Mary and cows and horses and real doves, roosters, shepherds and wise men...and...a baby called Jesus.

Belinda says we have to rest until 6pm. She eats a banana right in front of my wooden cot! She has no manners! I want her to share it with me, but I dare not ask. I can't sleep because I am too excited with anticipation. "Belinda, ich muss," I say hopefully, sensing this British woman will allow me to go to the outhouse even though I don't really need to "go." She doesn't buy it. I toss and turn. One hour is too long for a child to wait!

I hear faint singing wafting through the hot evening air. It's something about people looking east and making their homes fair. Then another song; this time it's louder:

> The stars shall light your journey;
> Your mother holds you close and warm;
> The donkey's pace shall rock you:
> Sleep baby; dream no harm.[4]

The angels lead the entire community—mothers, fathers, teens, Omas and Opas—into the Kindergarten, and we children get up from our cots and follow them. I easily find my family. Together the whole community walks up the tree-lined pathway, past the dining hall and the kitchen, down a sandy, tree lined road, to the cow and horse stalls.

We gather around the manger. Everything is real, just like the stories I have heard! Mary and Joseph have come a long way, and so have the shepherds and the angels. They have travelled very far, to visit us in hot and humid Paraguay. How they got here I do not know. A tall, bearded man with a serious looking face gets out a black book and reads something about a decree. I don't know what that is. He says there was no room at the inn, but all I have ever seen are thatched huts, and down here no one ever turns anyone away! Here, one offers strangers a guampa filled with mate or tereré.[5] That innkeeper must have been a very bad person!

The man reading from the black book goes on, but my attention is fixed on an unruly oxen. A shepherd, who resembles my brother—I can't be quite sure—leads him away, lest the animal hurt the baby. The Man with the beard reads something about shepherds in the fields, but now my eyes are glued to a pigeon, sitting on a rafter, above father Joseph! It lifts its tail and makes a Klecks—you know what I mean?—and

*Fros families in 1959 in Isla Margarita. Back row: Papa, Mama, Aunt Iet and Uncle Herman (Papa's brother). I am seated front left.*

the Klecks lands oh-so-close to Joseph! I want to tell my Papa, but he motions me to be quiet. Now we walk by Mary and Joseph and the baby, but not too close, and we sing a farewell song to them.

My family walks home and Papa and Mama tell us children to wait outside. It is twilight by now, and the fire flies are dancing all around. We catch them. They are big! We gently lay them upside down in the sand, and watch them as they try to right themselves. A little bell rings, and Mama opens the planked, wooden entry door of our house. We eagerly enter the family room! We unwrap gifts, one at a time, so that all can see each gift and say how wonderful it is! My little hands struggle to open a box, and Hänsel unsheathes his Dolch—a mean-looking hunting knife that troubles his Mama—and cuts the string. I lift off the lid and there, to my great astonishment, is a little guitar! Papa—has—made—me—a—guitar! It's only a banana box with a wooden board nailed on, with nylon strings strung to nails, but it sounds real to me and I am very happy!

Now Mama lights the candles on the tree and we sing more songs. We never tire of singing! Then, finally, Papa gets the pillowcase of cookies from its hiding place, and pours glasses of homemade wine. Tomorrow we'll hike in the jungle! In the evening there will be a special meal, a Liebesmal, and my Kindergarten group will perform a play. It's something about being alone in this dark world. I don't speak English very well, so I only get the role of a shepherd.

The Christmas celebration will linger until the Three Wise Men arrive on January the sixth! The adults say they will come from the village of Itacoruby riding on horses, but I don't know if that is true, because the stories I have heard say they ride camels. I think I'll put out some water for the camels and an orange for the Wise Men to share. Maybe King Melchior will leave me a cookie or a can of dulce de leche.[6]

# Travels with My Family

*Es ist für uns seine Zeit angekommen*
*Die bringt uns eine grosse Freud*
*Übers schneebeglänzte Feld*
*Wandern wir durch die weite, weisse Weld.*

*A time has come,*
*a time of greatest joy.*
*Over the snow-covered field,*
*we wander across the wide white world.*[1]

In 1959, I believe, the community experienced great change within its leadership and life. A decision was made that the Paraguayan communities would be shut down, and that all of us would be transferred to the communities in England and the United States. My family was sent to England, where a new community had been started in the early fifties. My eldest sister Irene who was still studying in Uruguay and engaged to be married did not come with us.

It was to be a very long journey for us. Since we had only known life in rural Paraguay with just occasional visits to the local town, we were very excited. We drove by dusty truck to the port "town" of Rosario and boarded an old river boat to Asunción. We had never seen city life or street lights or advertisements. I was fourteen years old, but I had never seen an asphalt road before. It was a thrill to see all of this. When we took a plane to England, I remember feeling so awed by it all. I had a window seat and was amazed at seeing Rio de Janeiro from above before landing on the first stage of our journey. Upon arriving in England, we were driven in a little car on asphalt roads—a first for me! We were not used to such speed, so I was very car sick.

By this time, my brother Hans had left the community, but he traveled with us to England. He soon left for London and met and married his girlfriend, Vera, but we did not go to the wedding. At that time, if a family member married outside of the community, you didn't bless that or visit them. We only met Vera some years later. Hans and Vera moved to Canada, and they went on to have four children. Vera has been a wonderful sister-in-law to me.

We lived in England for one year in a village called Gerrards Cross close to London. The community had purchased an old

*My GCE class on graduation day, 1960. I am seated front left.*

mansion there, a beautiful house called Bulstrode Park.[2] Its grounds had many trees from all over the world and a beautiful lake with rhododendrons all around. In spring, there were carpets of bluebells and daffodils in the meadows behind the mansion. For a teenage girl from the tropics who had never even seen a daffodil, this was awesome. Living there was a good experience for me, but not just because of the surroundings. I was able to go to school there and got very good grades in German, art, and English.

However, after a year, my family moved to Germany, and lived outside of community for a couple of years. It was a difficult time, but my parents were very faithful to care for us with the little money and few possessions they had. We lived in Germany near my Grandmother for two years. We had never lived outside of a sheltered community setting, so this was a very difficult time for us. We felt like fish out of water. For us children, we knew nothing about how the world worked. The clothes were different, and we didn't even know how to shop.

Papa, Mama, and Melchior had gone ahead of us girls into Germany to find a house. The only affordable house we could rent was a summer cottage situated on the bank of a very beautiful lake but was in a very dilapidated condition. It was owned by my father's employer and was about an hour away from Hamburg. Three walls of this summer house

*In 1960 the teens at the Bulstrode Bruderhof enjoyed an all-day outing. One of our challenges was to build a "people pyramid." I am in the second tier, second from right.*

*In 1961 from left: Susi-Lucia, Mechthild, me (seated) and Melchior. Our family lived for one year at the Bullstrode Bruderhof Community in England.*

had large glass windows—nice in the summer but bad for the winter—and the floors were rotting. In fact, the whole house was built around a pear tree, its branches growing into our living room! In the autumn, my brother Melchior used to climb on the roof and gather pears from the gutters, and Mama used them in one of her simple recipes: potatoes, pears, and bacon cooked and served as a thick soup.

Our new home had electricity, but there was no water heater. We had a little kitchen with no table space and only two small burners on the stove for a family of six. The kitchen was also the

*1961: Papa and Melchior (Mel) ice sledding on the Park Manhagen Lake*

entry to the house. Everything was crammed into two rooms. We three girls had our own room, and Mama and Papa slept in the living room with Mel in a little bed on the side. During the cold German winter, the only heating was a coal stove in the living room. I remember waking up in the morning to find my blanket was frozen!

We lived week by week. Because Papa and Mama could not get skilled jobs related to their training Papa worked in a factory an hour's train ride away. My older sister Mechthild worked in a children's home, and even young Melchior would help by selling newspapers. We all worked together to make a few pennies, scraping enough together to survive. There were times when we would not have enough money. Though Papa and Mama would sit at the kitchen table and count the few German marks that were left to see if we should buy milk or bread, we never went hungry. My parents trusted God and did everything possible with their meager income to care for us.

At sixteen, I worked at my first job in a children's orphanage. I could not go to high school there, as I did not have enough education, so I helped to help to earn money for the family. However, I found this job very

*1962: Park Manhagen, Ahrensburg, Germany. Pictured is the summer cottage our family rented for three years. The man in front, Mr. Hess, rented some rooms on the other end of this house. He managed to flee with his wife across the wall separating East and West Germany.*

*My mama, Susi, preparing a meal at our rental house at Park Manhagen. There was no kitchen, just a two-burner hot plate in the entry corridor.*

difficult because I had to live at the orphanage during the week. I was petrified, especially when I had to come home on my own at the end of the week in the dark. After a few months, I said, "I can't do this. Please let me come home." So I ended up looking after the home, cooking, cleaning the house, and doing the shopping, while my mother cleaned the house for the owner of our cottage.

Since I was the only one at home and the house was very secluded, it was one of the loneliest times in my life. Sometimes my imagination would run away with me and incredible fear would grip me because I had only known life within a close-knit Christian community. Being by myself, I would imagine men with guns behind trees and ghosts. Because I believed in God, sometimes I cried out to Jesus to help me.

As difficult as this time in our lives was, it brought the family together. Whereas in community life, where children were taken care of by others most of the time and we saw very little of our parents, now we suddenly had to live as a single unit family. We were always together for the evening meals, weekends, and all the holidays. Despite the hardships, I am so thankful for this time.

When we lived in West Germany for these two years, the country was still divided following World War Two. In those early 1960s, we witnessed the tragedy of the wall that was raised between East and West Berlin; our neighbors were refugees from Eastern Germany, which was then a highly oppressive communist state. They had fled under a barbed wire fence, even as the divide was being erected, and had narrowly escaped being shot to death. My brother Melchior recalls our mother lighting a candle at Christmas to remember those less fortunate who died trying to cross the East-West Divide.

*Our family was invited to Sunday afternoon tea in Grossmutti's outdoor garden. I am seated on the right, second from back*

We lived close to our grandmother, my mother's mother,

who we called Grossmutti. My grandfather had died in the War, and their youngest son had died on the Russian front. Before the War, she had also lost a daughter in childhood, Heilwig. (Mama named my eldest sister after her, Irene Heilwig.) Grossmutti had never seen her Fros grandchildren before, and mama had not seen her for over twenty years, so it was a very special joy for her to see us. She came up every week to visit us in our "summer hut." She was already an elderly lady, but she was a stout and strong woman. When we arrived, she helped us with things that we needed like blankets and pillows. She often made us apple and plum tarts, which we loved because, in the community, we got cake only for birthdays or weddings.

Grossmutti would invite us to her home on Sunday afternoons. In Paraguay, we just had metal plates and cups—usually beaten up since so many people used them—and ate with spoons. I don't remember having forks. So when she invited us, we had to learn to eat with porcelain cups, saucers, and plates, and you had a fork just for the cake, a spoon for the coffee, and another spoon for the sugar! Of course, the coffee spoon mustn't go in the sugar bowl!

Grossmutti was very particular in these things, but she loved us dearly, and we developed a close relationship with her. While we were in Paraguay, because of the rule of the common purse, we didn't always receive the gifts she sent us. They were sometimes given to the community, particularly things of value. My grandmother found this very difficult to understand. But she was so good to us, and it was a great time of being together with our extended family.

After two years in Germany, we returned to the Bruderhof. In September 1963, we moved to America and rejoined the Bruderhof church community in Norfolk, Connecticut. Sadly, we did not see Grossmutti again. My mother visited her when we heard she was ill, and some time later, we heard that she had died.

*From left: Susi-Lucia, me and Mechthild playing our recorders on a Sunday afternoon visit with my grandmother (Grossmutti), Vilhelmine Gravenhorst. Grandfather died of hunger during World War II.*

# The Father Calls

*Tanneken, will you follow Me come what may?*

Great excitement filled us all. With the help of the community in the United States, my father worked diligently on getting us the visas to enter. One week before departure time, I developed a severe case of mumps with a very swollen neck. We had heard that people who are sick may not travel abroad. I was so worried that the trip would have to be postponed because of me. Shortly before the departure day, we had to go once more to Hamburg to finalize our papers. I took a shawl and wrapped it around my neck, hoping not to be discovered that I had mumps. All went well with never a question asked.

We crossed the Atlantic Ocean on a small Dutch ship, the *Maasdam*. As we passed Ireland, we were caught in a severe storm for the first two days, and we girls were very sick. They gave us the best food; food I had never seen in my life, but I couldn't eat one spoonful. Finally the storms eased and the last few days were beautiful and calm, which we thoroughly enjoyed.

As we entered America, the Lord's hand really was on us. It was fall, and the country was ablaze with red, yellow, and russet brown leaves, especially those of the oak and maple trees. What an impact this had on me! We re-entered community life and received a great welcome with reconciliation. My brother Mel tells me my old friend Heidi had drawn a big mural of our family, even including Hänsel, who was still in England. My father and mother were again full members, and we as teenagers were fully accepted, so I was able to join in again with community activities. On weekends, I worked with the children and helped with the youth choir, music still being my main passion in life. It was like life had begun again for us. In a new country, I felt we were finally home.

*1963: My family was taken to the harbor in Rotterdam, Holland by my Uncle Kees (Papa's brother) and Aunt Ietje. Our family is ready to board the ship, Maasdam, for our 10-day trip to the United States. From left: me, Papa, Uncle Kees, Aunt Letje, Mama and my sisters: Susi-Lucia and Mechthild*

---

### A brief account about Uncle Kees' imprisonment in a concentration camp during World War II as told by his daughter Pat Fros, Tanneken's cousin.

"From what I can recall, Dad had taken a stand against Hitler, but it was never exactly clear how he did that. It has been said that he was arrested because of documents, pamphlets or something like that.

"Dad never talked about his concentration camp experience with us, and Mom reluctantly shared very little. I do remember her telling us that Dad was arrested at a train station—I don't know in what city—and transported to a concentration camp, but I'm unsure which one. Mom told us that he was at Oranienunburg, north of Berlin; however, that concentration camp closed in 1934 so I think it must have been Sachsenhausen, also situated north of Berlin.

"The only thing I know for sure is that Dad survived a concentration camp. At the end of the war he and some other "prisoners" left the camp by foot and walked to Holland, mostly during the night because it was not safe during the day. It must have been horrible, because some of the men died on the way "home." Only my dad and one other person survived. I remember Mom telling us that Dad suffered from terrible nightmares, kicking her in his sleep."

*1965: I am next to my large perennial flower bed on the day of my high school graduation in Winsted, Connecticut. My family was part of the Evergreen Bruderhof Community.*

I attended public high school, which was very difficult for me because of my primitive Paraguayan education. I was not equipped for the American school system. I didn't know any American history, not even who George Washington was! I had never answered things like true or false statements or multiple choice questions. I thank the Lord that the Bruderhof spoke to the school guidance counselor, asking him to help me and give me time. I started in eleventh grade, general track, with a great desire to study music. I did well in school through the extra help I received from teachers and the guidance counselor, and I moved up to college track, graduating with As and Bs.

At nineteen years of age, I became a student at Winsted Community College where I studied general arts with a minor in music, specializing in violin and music theory. This one-year course was a stepping-stone to a four-year degree course. I had to travel fourteen miles down the road to Winsted in a car provided by the community. It was on one of these car journeys that I reached one of the lowest points in my life.

I was known as the happy, joyful Tanneken, who loved to help others, but I had entered deep depression. In each life, there come times when we must go through a valley and our faith is tested. From the age of thirteen, I had a great sadness within me. Many times I found myself weeping desperately, but I didn't tell anyone. I felt so low that I wanted to take my own life, and I remember getting the temptation to drive down a deep ravine or crash with a truck just to end it all.

I find it hard to answer why I felt like this. There is often not a full answer, or we seek an answer by blaming others. For me, I must honestly say that although I grew up in a Christian community, I was not a Christian; I did not know Jesus personally. Even though I knew Bible stories, I did not know Jesus. I believe the emphasis of my religious training was focused on good works: helping each other and the poor and sharing all things in common. These are all very commendable, but they do not save us. Only faith in Jesus Christ, repentance of our sins, and being faithful until the end will save us.

In the community, we did have prayer meetings, but only the leader would pray; there was no open prayer in which others participated. I had never heard my mother or father pray publicly. Nor had I heard others pray besides the leaders. I respected those who prayed, but for me I did not know the God to whom they prayed, the God who answers prayer. As a young person, I remember willfully deciding that I would no longer pray to God or sing worship songs to the Lord Jesus. It was like a voice inside me was instructing me to do this. I would seal my lips when songs were sung praising Him, and I believe that was the door that allowed Satan to enter.

Many times I returned home from college weeping. My parents saw this, but I could not explain what was happening in me. I had not spoken with anybody at all about how I was feeling, not my mother or father, my brothers and sisters, or anyone in the community. I hid everything; I was so ashamed of how I was feeling. And then one day on my way home from college, I was about to end my life. As I look back, it reminds me of the demon called Legion who Jesus bade enter the herd of pigs, which then ran down a steep bank to their deaths in the lake.

When I reached the community, I ran to our home with great fear that these suicidal feelings would overpower me. On that day, thank Jesus, Father was home. I ran into the living room and cried, "Papa, if you do not do something, I will take my life." I was in such distress. My father was shocked; he had no idea what was going on for me. But my father had the courage to say, "Tanneken, we will go on our knees and we will ask God for help." It was the first time I heard him pray. He knew his daughter was in great peril, and he cried out to the One he knew could help. At that moment, because I made a confession and brought them into the light, the power of those suicidal feelings was broken.

My dear Papa died some years ago, and I know he is home with the Lord because of the prayer he was able to pray that day. I know he could not have done that without genuinely knowing the Lord. I want to encourage all fathers and mothers, if you are Christian, pray with your children. Let them hear your prayers. I am so thankful that my father had the courage to pray together with me, which was unusual in our community as far as I had experienced to that time.

But then Papa said I had to go and confess to the elders. That was the rule we lived by, and Papa always strived to obey the community's rules. I wish I had never had to go further than the confession to my father, but I obeyed him and went to the elders and confessed my thoughts of suicide. They were shocked, and the only counsel they gave me was to go to a psychiatrist. This was frightening for me. I knew little about medical terms, so I did not know what a psychiatrist was. But I obeyed and went for some months. Well, they analyzed me and made me write down all my dreams, draw pictures, analyze people in my life and I don't know what all, but I felt I found no help there. Dear reader, the best psychiatrist is Jesus Christ; the best counselor is Jesus Christ; the best comforter is Jesus Christ. I respect Christian counseling, but for me, I felt all was dealt with in that confession and prayer with my father.

It was such a strange thing, sitting there in the psychiatrist's dim office, being told that if I wanted to I could throw shoes or express my feelings however I wanted to. The most difficult thing was that I was not allowed to talk with my mother or anyone else, except the elder of the church, about these sessions. The other very difficult thing was that throughout that year, I was not allowed to be part of the community prayer group. This banned me from what I now believe is a vital source of support for one who is suffering with and tormented by suicidal thoughts. No one should ever be excluded from prayer, especially in their hour of deepest need. That is where our only help lies.

Yet, I believe this experience really launched me on a search for God. It was the foundation for my future walk in freedom with the Lord. But in hindsight, I feel I was still bound in religious legalism, thinking I needed to do good works and be a good person to be a Christian.

A year later, because I was then considered a young adult, the community made the next decision in my life. The Bruderhof felt very strongly that membership in the community is a serious adult decision. Being born in the community does not make one a lifetime member. Young people are expected to live for a time "outside," in order for them to be sure that community life is what they want.

I found this very hard, as it felt like I was being thrown out on my own without any support. It had felt somewhat similar when I attended public high school. The life we lived in the community was so sheltered that we became very dependent on the community. Everything "inside" was regimented and all decisions were made for us, so anything "outside" felt very threatening and frightening. Needless to say, it was a great shock when it came time to leave, even though I was a young adult.

It was decided that I should go to college because I loved music and also had a great desire to work with disabled children. I entered Danbury State College in Connecticut to study music education and become a music teacher. Violin was my major, but I also learned many other instruments. I had various scholarships and grants to help me through. It was a good program, which I enjoyed, and despite the hard times, I am grateful that I was able to have this opportunity. Music filled my whole time.

1970: My sisters—Susi-Lucia (left) and Mechthild (right)—and I (middle) are making straw Christmas stars in our home in Winsted, Connecticut.

However, my spiritual life was still at a low ebb. The Bruderhof said that I had to stand "on my own feet." That meant that at first I could not go home to visit on weekends or special occasions. In fact, I only remember visiting the community twice through all those college years. I felt very alone. I had no friends or family near, and I had no Christian fellowship. I did have a Bible, but I only saw it as a book to tell me what to do when I was in trouble. For instance, if I was under church discipline, I felt I had to look to the Bible to learn how to fix things or put things right. I was ashamed of being seen reading the Bible because that would mean that I was in trouble, so I hid it under my pillow so my roommates did not see me reading it. And yet, because of my deep Christian foundation, I felt I lived a protected moral life during my college years. I did not enter into some of the things that other students did, such as drugs or alcohol, even though my inner life was empty.

The students at Danbury State College were so liberal that it made it difficult for me to join in and make friends. My background was so different. I was still wearing my Bruderhof clothing with my long community dress that had to be ten inches from the ground! Of course, I wanted to be accepted, but I had to keep myself apart in many

In 1970 I graduated from Danbury State College, Danbury, Connecticut with a BS in music education. Mama is on the left.

ways, as I lived in fear that I would not be allowed to return to the community. I had roommates, but I didn't socialize with them.

However, I did make one friend, Sarah. She was an unhappy girl and was very lonely, having come from a difficult family background. I believe God gave me a heart of compassion for her. We listened to music together and both played in the college orchestra. Sarah played the French horn beautifully, which probably helped her self-esteem. Over the years, I saw a definite change in her, so I think I helped her even as she helped me.

Sometimes I had to take a stand in face of the liberalism around me. Though I wasn't a Christian "by faith" yet, I still lived according to the Christian values I'd been taught. In a psychology class, we were shown videos of naked people, which to me appeared to be pornography and repugnant. I refused to attend the class, risking failing the subject and had to explain myself to my professor. Thank Jesus, when I took the exam, I scraped by with a C. However, despite such incidents, my primitive Paraguayan education, and only two years of American high school, I had an A average when I graduated. Praise the Lord! And, my dear Mama was with me when I graduated. I am so thankful to the Lord for the opportunity the Bruderhof community gave me to attend college.

Yet, my college years were fraught with hardship and lessons to learn outside the classroom. I had to work during college, and one summer went to work as an assistant cook in a Jewish summer camp. We worked very hard; I was mainly responsible for bakery and salads. We didn't have recipes so I had to think on the spot, and we were way understaffed. I must have lost twenty pounds that summer. The Jewish head cook liked me very much, I think, because I was jovial, a people pleaser, didn't complain, and was a hard worker. We talked a lot, but I didn't think anything of this; he was married and had a beautiful wife and children. At the same time, a worker on the grounds asked me out for supper. I was so naïve. I asked him what for; I didn't realize he was asking me for a date! Of course, I had to say no. Dating was against community rules, and I so desperately wanted to get back into the community.

I continued to get on well with the head cook, and he would say sweet things to me and touch me on the shoulder. I guess he was flirting with me, but I didn't realize this for such things did not happen in the community. I knew nothing at all about sex at that time. One day, as we were chatting, I sat on his lap. He drew me in, and I willingly went, but that was as far as it went. I guess I was hungry for friendship and acceptance. But suddenly I realized what was happening, cut the whole thing off, and became very grouchy around him. I was so scared that I had sinned by sitting on his lap. I called the elder from the community and confessed what I had done. He, together with my mother, actually visited me, which rarely had happened before. He was very strict with me, telling me this must never happen again.

During these years, my parents also left the community for a time. The reasons for this are their story, not mine. This time the family was split apart. Mama and Papa moved out with my brother Mel, leaving us three sisters in the community but attending college. Each one of us lived "outside" as our time came.

My brother Mel had been losing his hearing since our stay in Germany, and now it decreased even further. One day while on a bus with Mama, he suddenly said, "Mama, I cannot hear anything," and from that moment on was completely deaf. I wasn't present at that time, but I believe Mel suffered greatly, and Mama and Papa had to carry this burden of worry and care very much alone. Sadly, I don't think my sisters and I were a good moral support for my parents and Mel then. It was a time of division within the family, and I felt very split inside as well.

Towards the end of college, I was eventually allowed to visit the community on weekends. I was not a member yet, but I could participate in "non-membership" meetings. This made me feel awkward; I was in the community where I had grown up but felt like an outsider. It was a strange feeling, I don't know if that makes sense, and yet I was happy that I

*My brother Hänsel (Hans) and I are relaxing during a holiday in St. Williams, Ontario, Canada.*

*Deer Spring Community youth group in 1973. I am third from the right in row three. My brother Melchior (Mel) is at the back to the right of the window.*

was being allowed to draw back into the community, bit by bit, which was where I so wanted to be.

After these visits, on my way back to college or work, I visited my parents and Mel. Each time, I excitedly told them the community news and what had happened on the weekend. My mother and father wanted to hear all about it. Mother did not seem well; her head was always cast down. I felt sad to see my mother like this; I have no idea what she went through. They returned to the community after six years and lived the rest of their lives as part of the Bruderhof. Mel returned for two years after college, but soon left and joined a community of his own choice.

In the midst of all this, I heard the voice of God. I cannot put a date on it exactly, but I remember the experience as if it were an hour ago. I was in a prayer meeting in the community's dining room, probably during a weekend or holiday visit. God spoke to me, "Tanneken, will you follow Me come what may?"

I did not respond directly at that time. I did not truly know it was God's voice, not understanding that God could speak in this way so directly to an individual. Only later on I remembered this experience and understood its significance for me. I'm still amazed that God clearly spoke to a little Bruderhof girl of no importance in the world. I did not know Jesus as I know Him now, but I did try to obey and follow Him as best I could within the community setting. I did not know how hard this would be to obey in the years ahead, but I would hear Him ask this again and again.

# Trying to Belong

*For He shall give His angels charge over you, to keep you in*
*all your ways. In their hands they shall bear you up,*
*lest you dash your foot against a stone.*
Psalm 91:11-12

After I graduated, I wrote to the community and asked if I could come back home. They said, "No, it is now best if you go and find a job; you are not spiritually ready to come back." I was devastated. I was so desperate to be baptized into the community, but I could not attain what seemed to be impossibly high standards. Little did I know then that God was preparing me to become a follower of Jesus Christ, free of human bondage and fear to follow the Lord's plan for my life, wherever it led.

I went to work in Hartford, Connecticut, in a day care center in one of the poorest areas of the city, working with African American and Puerto Rican children. I chose this job purposely because I'd always wanted to work with the poorest of the poor. Other than the director, I was the only white member on staff. I think I chose to work in this area partly to show I didn't agree with racism, which was a new thing for me. I was appalled that people suffered because of the color of their skin. But because of my sheltered upbringing, I didn't always know that certain things were racist. I got into trouble one day for calling a child "boy," not understanding its segregationist history. But I learned and greatly valued my time there.

The conditions and the resources at the center were very poor. Rats crawled out of the floorboards, and I had to be creative to provide materials for craft projects or homemade musical instruments. There was also a high level of crime in that particular neighborhood. One day at work, the alarm went off, and we were told there was a man in the building with a knife. We had to get all the children out quickly, but thankfully, we were all kept safe that day.

I lived with my sisters, Mechthild and Susi-Lucia, who were also "outside" the community. It was good to be with them, but each of us was occupied with our job. I always traveled to work by public transport, often in the dark, and I felt the hand of the Lord upon me in some dangerous situations. One day, while waiting at the bus stop close to the day care center, three young men surrounded me, verbally abusing me because I was white. They wanted to trip me up, and if they had, I would have been in great danger. But they could not do it. I remained calm and did not respond to their taunts. I felt encircled by angel wings. I actually felt them and knew that God was protecting me. The men went away, and I was safe. I can only think now of Psalm 91, where it speaks of God commanding His angels to guard us, so that we will not even strike our foot against a stone. Even though I did not really know God at that time, He was there, sending His angels to guard me.

Another time at night, I was returning from the local library. I walked up to our house singing a praise song. As I neared the door, I felt a hand moving up my leg under my dress. A man was lying just beneath me. I wanted to scream for help, but I could not; my voice was frozen. Then the man got up, grinned at me in an evil, lustful way, and ran off. As I look back, again I know that the protecting hand of the Lord was upon me because if anything had happened, I would not have been able to defend myself.

After two years of working at the center—feeling scared of traveling there after the things that had happened—once again I wrote and asked if I could return to the community. I was told, "Not yet." It was a great disappointment to me. I worked for a while in the kitchen of a factory producing alcohol. It was a terrible place to work with pictures of naked women on the walls and a lot of rough talk. I tried to live a good Christian life there, but it was just too much for me. I wrote to the community yet again, asking to return, and after a few months, the community finally said yes, and I was allowed to go home. My parents had also returned, so it was a great joy to be back with them after so many years. Mechthild and Susi-Lucia returned some years after me, and both have remained in the community until today.

Melchior also returned for a few short years, and I, more than my sisters, learned to help him communicate and interpret for him at community meetings. Eventually, we learned some basic signing.

Those last years were not easy for Mel, so he left the community in 1975, in part because of the injustices he saw.

I still had a heart to follow God and to do what was right. I was keen to follow Him wherever He led as He had asked me some years before, but the only way I knew was through the Bruderhof life. So I asked to be baptized and was taken into the Novitiate. This is the first step in committing your whole life to God through life in the community. It includes taking very serious vows to be faithful to the community to the end of your life, to surrender all personal belongings, to put yourself completely at the disposal of the community, and to accept every admonishment given by the leadership, as well as being prepared to admonish others. It is a kind of testing period, after which the elders may agree for you to be baptized and welcomed as a full member of the community. I took the vows and entered the Novitiate, hoping that in the future I would be able to be baptized.

All this I did out of fear and the need to be accepted by the "in" group, because I was tired of being sent away and unwanted. In retrospect, after I was born again in Jesus years later, I could see that I had bound myself more to man than to God when I made those vows. This was perhaps not the community's intention, but I believe it was my experience, so though I was now finally accepted by the community, I was, in actuality, in bondage to the fear of man.

For a year or two things seemed to go well. At first I worked with the children and was active in the youth group. I taught violin, led the children's choir, and played in the community orchestra. But I was told I was too proud of my musical abilities, and so I had to give up all work in the music field. I did participate in a string quartet, however, which brought me great relief. I was allowed to continue working with children for about two years, but not to teach music.

Then a second period of depression came, although this time I was not suicidal. I think my difficulty was that I was not being accepted for who I was. I begged to be baptized into the community, but it was not allowed. One's thought life was a big issue, and I felt compelled to confess all my "evil" thoughts: my anger against the elders or jealousy of other families. Some of them really were not worth confessing, and yet I felt bound to. I did not understand that Jesus loves me as I am though others could not. So I confessed everything and was put under church discipline.

Around this time, I stopped working with children and began working in the laundry and the children's kitchen. In general, jobs were assigned by the work distributor as was needed without favoritism or personal preference influencing the distributor's choices. However, since I was depressed over no longer working with children or the music I loved, I believed that the menial jobs, such as cleaning toilets, were always given to those under some form of church discipline, so I didn't have the best attitude. I cleaned, cooked, and sewed clothes. I particularly enjoyed working in the children's kitchen, cooking for over a hundred children, and in the sewing room, where I made skirts and blouses. Now I know that God uses all experiences for good and can see that everything I learned to do in those years helped me in my future life.

A great pain for me was not being allowed to attend the common prayer meetings. When under church discipline, you had to sit in a separate room, listening to the meeting over a loudspeaker. Finally, even though I had taken the novice vows, I confessed my anger at some of the elders' actions towards others and was taken out of fellowship. It was decided I must leave community life once more. I firmly believe now that this is what God allowed so that I could come into a true faith and trust relationship with the Lord.

I remember well the day I packed my suitcase. It was a cold winter morning in February 1979. I wept so much that the tears dripped down into my suitcase. I didn't yet know it, but this was to be the final separation from my family and my home within the community. It was one of the lowest points of my life. My mother was in the home, but stood at a distance, watching me pack. Surely my mother must have felt pain as she watched me, weeping, getting ready to leave, but what could she do or say? Mama asked me, "What is your favourite song?" I answered, "Leave It in the Hands of the Lord."

> Chorus:
> Do not worry over what to eat,
> What to wear or put upon your feet.
> Trust and serve and do your best today
> Then leave it in the hands of the Lord,
> Leave it in the hands of the Lord.
>
> Verse:
> The Lord knows all your needs,
> He knows before you ask.
> So only trust in Him for He will do the task

Of bringing to your life whatever you must know.
He'll lead you through the darkness wherever you must go.

Chorus:
Do not worry over what to eat,
What to wear or put upon your feet.
Trust and serve and do your best today
Then leave it in the hands of the Lord,
Leave it in the hands of the Lord.

We sang as I packed my suitcase, yet I felt very much alone. I can see now that God was with me, promising His care and protection through this song. I feel very much that, like Corrie Ten Boom, this was the moment when my "tramping for the Lord" began, following Him "come what may."

# Finding Christ

*"We're from your Flock, Jonathan. We are your brothers."*
*The words were strong and calm. "We've come to take you*
*higher, to take you home"..."Home, I have none. Flock I*
*have none. I am Outcast. And we fly now at the peak of*
*the Great Mountain Wind. Beyond a few hundred feet, I*
*can lift this body no higher"..."But you can, Jonathan.*
*For you have learned. One school is finished,*
*and the time has come for another to begin."*
From "Jonathan Livingston Seagull"[1]

In this period of being sent away, I was very alone. At first I was not permitted to return to the community on weekends, birthdays, or holidays. I went to work in a home for severely disabled children as a classroom aid. As I started this position, I was still wearing my Bruderhof clothing, my long dress, long-sleeved blouse, and a blue head scarf, which indicated I was currently under church discipline.

In the months that followed, a new friend, Pat Ahnrud, gave me the book *Jonathan Livingston Seagull*. It helped me in transitioning from dependence upon the community to life on my own. I had to learn to rent an apartment, pay bills, and go daily to work on my bicycle, this time without the support of my sisters. Though I was only earning minimum wage, whatever I had left over I sent to the community. I was still under the Novice vows that required me to hand over everything to the common purse. I don't know how I did it, but somehow I managed to live with the minimal necessities.

I was bound to sadness, fear, rejection, insecurities, feelings of abandonment, no family, no friends, very alone, and facing dangers. In a critical and judgmental way, I compared everything about community life to life on the "outside." The small book about a seagull finding his own way while being excluded from his own flock gave me courage to loosen the chains that bound me and walk in a freedom I had never known.

But I had a long way to go. I remember my brother Mel inviting me to his wedding. He had been out of the community for some years then and had met Janet in an audiology clinic. I had had very little contact with him, afraid that if the community found out, it could affect my being able to return. So I refused because of the community's views of marrying "outside." This must have been very painful to him and something I deeply regret. I missed a great opportunity to show love to my brother. But later, I was able to ask forgiveness from him, and he and Janet have continued to be a wonderful support to me.

Pat was the director of the education program for the disabled children, and I worked with her in her classroom. At first, I was very shocked and found working with such severely disabled children very hard. I had never seen such impairments, and I found it very upsetting, to the point of tears. But Pat, even though she was in charge, exercised these children and cleaned them up; nothing was too much trouble for her. Her love for the children was a great example to me. I began to use music as therapy and sang songs that motivated the children to move and sway and exercise. I also used it to teach simple mathematics; for instance, I used a drum beat to teach them how to count. Looking back, I can see how the Lord was beginning to develop my vocation in working with "the least of these My brethren" (Matt. 25:40.)

Even in my free time, I was involved with activities for the children. I worked with Pat to develop summer camps for them. At that time, summer camp programs were mainly aimed at able-bodied children, and disabled children did not have many opportunities. We worked on this for some years along with young people from her church.

Pat was a devoted Christian. I thank the Lord for this woman of God, who wanted so much to fellowship with other Christians. She invited me many times to go to church. And many times I refused. Still bound to my community vows, I was not free to pray or worship with others, only with the Bruderhof. I was very scared to do anything that might prevent my return home or cause me to be finally cut off. In spite of the estrangement that I began to feel toward the community, a yearning was still in me to be with my family there.

Yet Pat was very patient with me. She invited me to her home and cooked me lovely meals. She asked me to say thank you to God together with her for the meal, but I refused. This hurt her very deeply; she could not understand why I couldn't pray with her. She knew by my dress and my behavior that I was "religious," so my refusal to say grace at a meal must have seemed inexplicable. I found out later that Pat always prayed for me, interceding for me to our dear Father in Heaven.

One Easter vacation, I was not allowed to go home, and of course, I could not go to church anywhere else, so I just sat in my apartment. Pat had invited me to go to church with her, but as before, I refused. So she left me an Easter lily with a precious note that read in part: "The God you love is the God I love too. May He go before you; may He go after you. May He be behind you, may He be on each side of you." It was written with such love and forgiveness! This was the first time I had heard there was a personal God going before you, going after you, and looking after you. Could it be that God cared for just one little person like me?

We became good friends and went on many camping trips together. She continued to invite me to church, and I consistently refused. We gradually developed a routine on a Sunday morning where she would pick me up and drop me off in a park in Pittsfield, Massachusetts, while she went off to church. After she picked me up, we had lunch together before she took me home. Once in a while, she would play Christian music tapes in her car, which was very new to me. Of course, we sang worship songs in the community, but very few expressed a relationship with Jesus. I liked these new worship songs very much; something moved deep within my spirit as I heard them, but I didn't say anything for fear that someone in the community might find out.

Finally, I decided to buy a little radio. In the community, we had no television or radio; news of current events outside the community was reported at common meals. I bought the radio with much trepidation; I really thought that to own a radio was sinful, especially because the money I spent on it was supposed to go back to the community. But I bought it, not knowing that God was working in me, preparing the way, using this means to bring me to salvation.

I started to listen to Christian radio stations. I had no prayer life and read the Bible very little. Today I daily read the Word – it is my bread, my counsel, my delight – but at that time I did not see it as such. Often in the car, Pat would listen to the Lutheran hour, preached by a Pastor Yingling, of St Paul's Lutheran Church, in Albany. He preached every Sunday, and preached only the word of God. In my room I secretly tuned in, and listened intently. I was starting to hear the gospel; that we are saved by grace, and not by works. As I listened to these messages, a new faith was being birthed in me. I shared with Pat that

I was listening to Christian radio, and that I liked what I was hearing. She thought that was the same as going to church, but I was still too afraid to do that. But I was beginning to listen to God in my inner ear, and my bondage to man's ideas was loosening.

By hearing the truth of God's word my wrong understanding of the Bible was taken away. I was starting to "hear" the Gospel in a new way. I will never forget when pastor Yingling preached on Ephesians 2:4-10:

> But God, who is rich in mercy, because of His great love with which He loved us, even when we were dead in trespasses, made us alive together with Christ (by grace you have been saved), and raised us up together, and made us sit together in the heavenly places in Christ Jesus, that in the ages to come He might show the exceeding riches of His grace in His kindness towards us in Christ Jesus. For by grace you have been saved through faith, and that not of yourselves; it is the gift of God, not of works, lest anyone should boast. For we are His workmanship, created in Christ Jesus for good works, which God prepared beforehand that we should walk in them.

Chains fell off! I was being freed to know and believe that we are saved by grace. I started to understand that good works are a *result* of our salvation, not the *means* to salvation.

One evening before Christmas, I was at Pat's listening to Christmas music. Pat told me later she felt a demonic force present and had to go to her room to intercede for me. The song "Away in a Manger" came on, and I knelt in her living room as I listened to it. Suddenly, I felt free from whatever tormented me. I sang the whole song; it was the third verse that was key:

> Be near me, Lord Jesus, I ask Thee to stay
> Close by me forever, and love me, I pray.
> Bless all the dear children in Thy loving care
> And fit us for Heaven to live with Thee there.

When I finished singing to myself and my Jesus, Pat came from the kitchen, looked into the door, and said, "Now you have done it; you have accepted Jesus." Though this brought me so much closer to a relationship with Jesus, God knew I wasn't quite there yet. He saw in my heart that there was still a barrier He had to deal with.

One Sunday sometime later, I was alone in my room listening to the Lutheran hour. Pastor Yingling was preaching on the humility of the publican and the pride of the Pharisee in Luke's gospel[2]. He talked about the Pharisaic spirit in each one of us that we must overcome. Suddenly, tears rolled down my cheeks. I knew I had a Pharisaic spirit. I judged everybody—everybody who didn't live in the community, who didn't wear a head covering or a long dress, who didn't understand pacifism or living by the common purse. This spirit was the barrier keeping me apart from a relationship with Jesus, and God was dealing with it.

As the message ended, I wept; I was so sorry for how judgmental I had been. I prayed to God for forgiveness. This was the moment when I was born again, where I repented and called out to God. I did not understand the concept of being born again then, but God was working in my life, bringing me to Him. I told Pat about this and she simply said, "Now we can fellowship together." Yet, I was bound by fear, the fear of being cut off from the community. It took some time before the Lord released me from my fears and I was able to go to church.

One Sunday, a storm blew up, which prevented Pat from dropping me off by a lake, so she took me to church and left me in the car. Our friend Kay asked me why I was sitting outside alone and wouldn't come into church. I was reluctant to explain myself but told her I couldn't yet pray with other Christians. Then Kay said something very special and important, "Tanneken, don't you know that all of us are Christians who believe in Jesus, and we are in this church to worship Him? We ask forgiveness, as all of us are sinners, and we need His grace." Because I had been excluded from the community prayer meetings so many times, this was the first time in my life that I heard I could go to church as a sinner. I believed I was never good enough, and now I began to understand I could approach God, as a sinner, through my beloved Savior Jesus Christ.

The chains were broken, and I started to go to church faithfully every Sunday. I spoke to the pastor and shared with him a little of who I was and of my background, still in part out of fear that I was not good enough. He said, "Come and fellowship with us." It was a deep experience for me. Every Sunday, I grew more and more in my faith in Jesus through the sermons and worship. I began to see that the body of Christ is bigger than any one community; that it was made up of many communities, churches, and denominations. I finally began to take communion, something I had never been able to do as an un-baptized member in the community. None of us are worthy of communion, but if we believe in Jesus Christ and have repented of our sins, we can commune with Him. This was so special for me.

I still had many things that the Lord needed to deal with in my life. Pat was with me as I dealt with all these things, and I think she got very frustrated with me sometimes! For instance, I still wore the head covering of the community. It was very important to me. In a sense, I was trusting in it and judging others for not wearing it. On a camping trip, Pat saw me taking it off. After folding it very gently and placing it next to me, she dared to say, "You know, that head covering is more important to you than the Bible."

I finally decided not to wear it any more. I understand those who do it out of obedience to Scripture[3] and respect that, but in my case, it became such a judgmental issue that I had to let it go. I began to read Christian testimonies and biographies. As I read Corrie Ten Boom's book, *Tramp for the Lord,* and realized that her prayers were answered without wearing a head covering, I began to be freed to follow the Lord as He showed me. But it was a long time before I could give up my long skirts.

I remember another Sunday evening when I was still struggling over being shunned and kept out of the community. I had come home after a conversation with Pat, who was trying to help set me free from my critical and judgmental thoughts toward other Christians. I left confused and upset. As I went to turn off the light, I found a piece of paper under my door, which I found out later Pat had left. She had written down a song I had never heard before; it calmed me and later became one of my favorites.

> Like the woman at the well, I was thirsting
> For things that could not satisfy,
> And then I heard my Savior speaking,
> Draw from the well that never will run dry.
> Fill my cup, Lord, I lift it up, Lord,
> Come and quench the thirsting of my soul.
> Bread of Heaven, feed me 'til I want no more;
> Fill my cup, lift it up and make me whole.[4]

By then I had started reading the Bible, so I found this story in John 4. Jesus dealt with this lady one-on-one and met her where she was at. He alone knew what her deepest need was. She came to faith in Jesus right away and immediately became an evangelist

1980: I am celebrating with Daniel (severely disabled mentally and physically) his birthday at the Vesper Hill Residential Program for the Disabled in Great Barrington, Massachusetts.

for the Lord's gospel. "And many of the Samaritans of that city believed in Him because of the word of the woman who testified, 'He told me everything I *ever* did'" (John 4:39).

Jesus accepted her and did not dwell on the sin she had committed. He did not go to the synagogue or a membership meeting, nor did He go to the market place or a place of public information and tell everyone what she had done. In fact, He told no one else but spoke into her life, lovingly exposing the truth of what she did and letting her know that He was the Messiah, the one she and all of Israel was waiting for. Only the Lord could transform and fill her thirsting soul for He said, "But the water that I shall give him will become in him a fountain of water springing up into everlasting life" (John 4:14). He alone could fill what her hungering soul needed; in the same way, only Jesus could fill my thirsting soul and calm my need to be accepted and never more rejected.

## From Pat Davenport (formerly Pat Ahnrud) former special needs teacher and long time friend

I was working at Vesper Hill Nursery School in Great Barrington when Tanneken came to work there. This was a residential facility for 110 severely, profoundly disabled children. Tanneken arrived one day saying she needed to work in a pacifistic organization. Her attire was quite unusual for staff people and we all wondered where she had come from. She was dressed in a long out-dated dress with a kerchief on her head. She spoke with quite a German accent. She was a diligent worker, but did not have any friends on the job and was very quiet and withdrawn. I invited her to go for supper several times, and in our conversations, she was able to say that she was placed in this institution to work because of behavior in the community. She further said that she was seeking baptism, and the community did not think she was ready for it. I did not ask any other questions.

As time went on, I invited her to go to church with me, but she said that she could not. This would be against the community rules. I continued to invite her to other social events and to be with my other Christian friends. She was always reluctant to share or talk about her faith. At the table, she would not say grace.

One Advent evening in winter, she came to my apartment and we just meditated and listened to some Christian music. All of a sudden, I felt a compelling force that was frightening. I had never experienced that before. It penetrated the room and I had to run away. I ran to my bedroom and fell on my knees in prayer. I prayed that the evil one would leave. I can't remember the details after that. I don't know if Tanneken came into the room and I shared with her what had happened or if I went to the living room to tell her about this. She was very quiet about it all when I told her.

After that experience, I invited her to go to church with me again and she agreed to go but she would sit in the car and wait for me to come out. I always listened to a Christian radio station with a Pastor Yingling from Albany preaching. I told Tanneken that I wanted her to be quiet as we traveled. It was about twenty-seven miles. I told her that this man of God always had something that I could relate to in my daily walk and just maybe he would speak to her too if she were quiet.

Some time after these Sundays, she told me that she had called Pastor Yingling. He heard her story as she asked for baptism. He addressed her as, "my sister," and these words spoke loudly to her as this was what the community called each other. She went to Albany to meet with this pastor and they set a time for her to be baptized. She told me about it, and we were so excited. I invited all our Christian contacts to come on her day to witness the event.

## From Kay Moldenke
## former Bible teacher and long time friend

I think I met Tanneken at a picnic at Pontoosac Lake when she came with Pat. I was caring for my mother at the time, and we went there often for lunch or supper. It was such a beautiful setting looking out over the lake and to the Berkshire hills. I knew Tanneken was working with special needs children and that she loved music—interests I shared.

Tanneken was gracious and caring for my mother. I knew nothing of the Bruderhof community then, but do remember that Tanneken was wearing a head scarf and long dress at the time. That seemed to be her identity. I felt she was searching and seeking for something but couldn't quite put my finger on it. She seemed very set in her ways, legalistic, bound, at times judgmental, and I couldn't break through the facade.

I remember her being in Pat's car when Pat and I met at our church for Sunday worship one Lord's Day. (We were probably picnicing after the service.) I invited Tanneken to join us in worship, and she refused rather self-righteously, as I recall. It was as though entering a church was somehow sinful and verboten [forbidden]. I don't remember exactly what I said to her, but I probably asked her whether she felt she was better than other people! Not the most gracious response on my part! But I'm sure I added something to the effect that the church was for sinners, and that I was one of them, but a forgiven sinner cleansed by the blood of the Lord Jesus. (I NEED the church, the Body of Christ with whom I can freely worship and sing His praises and with whom I can kneel around the Table; I need the church where I can hear the Word preached in power and where I can be equipped for service and encouraged on my journey. It was inconceivable to me that anyone who professed Christ would not feel the same way.) I simply did not understand where Tanneken was coming from. The fault was mine, not Tanneken's.

I will never forget the day before Mama died. It was just a few days before Christmas, and Tanneken visited her and they sang together "Alle Jahre Wieder," a German Christmas song. The very next evening while I was at a Bruderhof community Christmas program with Pat in Rifton, New York state, my dear Mama passed into Glory. According to Pat, Tanneken was not with us; we had been invited by another community member who worked with Pat. We both remember that it was a very special program with angels flying around in the "heavens" and beautiful music, of course, which is a community forte. We lingered afterward and interacted with members of the community—very warmly received.

When Pat dropped me off at my mother's apartment around 11 p.m., I found my mother on the floor. While the angels were singing at Rifton, others had come to take my dear Mama Home. Tanneken lovingly made a Christmas wreath, covering it with tiny red and white paper stars that she handcrafted in the German fashion. I considered it a final gift of love for my mother. It is a testimony to Tanneken's utter selflessness today that she has totally forgotten this.

Yes, today Tanneken is totally the opposite of the young woman I first met— she is free, open, accepting, alive in the Spirit, joyful, totally in love with Jesus, totally committed to giving her life for the sake of the Gospel and her precious orphans in Mozambique. I think Tanneken herself would say, "Once I was blind but now I see! Hallelujah!" And the Spirit continues His work within her and through her to the saving and blessing of countless lives. Tanneken truly is a new creation in Christ—the difference between night and day.

# Baptized into God's Family

*I have every confidence that by the grace of God,*
*Tanneken will go on her way this day*
*and always rejoicing in the Lord.*
Pastor Stanton Yingling
at Tanneken's baptism service

While still living in the community, God had spoken to me, asking me to follow Him wherever He led. I did not know then that it would be at the cost of everything—leaving home, family, friends, and the church community life that was my security. My decision to be baptized "outside" would mean being expelled from the community forever. Yet, I could not ignore the deep desire within me to leave it all and follow Jesus.

I decided to call Pastor Yingling, whose sermon on the radio had brought me to repentance and faith, and request baptism in Christ. I arranged to visit him and made the journey to Albany on public transport. I confessed to him my previous spiritual pride and requested baptism. We continued to correspond, and he agreed to baptize me at his church.

In the fervor of my new found faith, I wrote to my parents and the community, asking forgiveness for anything I had done to offend them and inviting them to my baptism. I told them about the Christian friends I had found, wonderful godly people who I could pray and fellowship with. I guess I had some hope they would understand, but they didn't. The elder of the community wrote and informed me that I was no longer part of their community, and that I could have no more contact with them nor enter their grounds. They only wanted to hear from me if I were seriously ill. Since I had taken the novice vows, to their understanding, I was unfaithful to what I had promised. I don't remember hearing from my parents over this.

I had indeed "left it all" to follow Jesus. However, I remain eternally thankful for my upbringing by my parents and the community. Though I did not find a personal relationship with Christ through the community, yet the many years I spent with the Bruderhof—fifteen in Paraguay, one in England, and my sixteen interrupted years in America—deeply implanted in me what it means to be a disciple of Jesus and how the Christian faith can be lived out in love to God and to your neighbor. I know that sounds strange to some given the experiences I have described, but the community did exemplify God's love in many ways, and that lifestyle kept me protected and morally pure.

I still did not understand the purpose of having to be separated from my family and the fellowship of my brothers and sisters in the community. However, I have learned to forgive. I know that God understands and knows all, and everything He allows He can turn to good. With all that I have come through, I always fall back on God's question to me, and to this day, I have continued to answer, "Yes, I will follow You come what may." I can only rejoice in the Lord in how He has seen me through the good times as well as the very, very difficult times.

I was baptized at St. Paul's Lutheran Church in Albany on the 19th of June, 1983 at thirty-seven years old. My parents and my sisters were not there, but my dear brother Mel and his wife Janet came even though just two years before I had refused to go to their wedding. I asked Pastor Yingling if I could be baptized in a lake in one of the Albany parks, but since he had suffered a severe heart attack, it was too much for him, so we agreed to do it as part of the Sunday morning worship service. My true baptism had taken place in my heart, so the form in which I was baptized did not matter so much to me. He quoted one of my letters to him at the service:

> My heart is filled with praise and thanks to God for His endless mercy and love and His guidance through you. It moves me and challenges me how you and how all at St. Paul's are reaching out to me in Christian love at this special time in my life. I feel so unworthy of all this, but I am so thankful to you for this time of preparation for baptism.
>
> I also want to share with you that the passage in Acts 2:35-39 has meant and still means so much to me, where Peter and the apostles, filled with the Holy Spirit, testified to and proclaimed the risen Lord. Peter said, "Let all Israel accept as

certain, that God has raised this Jesus, whom you crucified, both Lord and Messiah." And further on, "'Repent,' said Peter, 'repent and be baptised every one of you, in the name of Jesus, Messiah, for the forgiveness of your sins, and you will receive the gift of the Holy Spirit.'"

This passage cut me to the heart, and I pray to God for mercy, that I in my sinful life caused that same dreadful suffering that Jesus endured on the cross for my sins.

After explaining the purpose of baptism, Pastor Yingling asked me, "Sister Tanneken, Jesus is asking you, who do you say that He is?"

I answered, "I believe that Jesus is the Son of the living God, that He died for my sins, and on the third day, He rose again and is living now. He is my only God to live for."

A second question followed. "You have heard the good news, the gospel of Jesus Christ. You have heard God's invitation to you. What is your desire?"

I replied, "It is my desire as a sinner who just asks for God's mercy to be baptized for the forgiveness of sins and be baptized into Christ, in His Church, and to follow Him for the rest of my life, come what may."[1] On my confession, Pastor Yingling baptized me with a simple sprinkling of water on my forehead. I remember the loud applause

*I was baptized in Albany, New York in 1982. Front row, from left: me, Pastor Yingling and his wife and Pat Ahnrud Davenport. Second row: Kay Moldenke (behind me), my brother Melchior (Mel) (center) and his wife Janet (behind him)*

as we ended the ceremony, very unusual in a Lutheran church at that time. After the service, we celebrated in the basement of the church; they had even made me a "birthday" cake, a happy born-again birthday cake.

As we later took communion, the hymn was sung, "Just as I am, without one plea...O Lamb of God, I come, I come." This hymn came to me as healing balm after being "tossed about with many a conflict, many a doubt." I was desperate for Jesus and came to Him by faith upon His invitation, not upon merit of my own. I could come to Jesus and was accepted by my Beloved without pre-determined rules, religious clothing, or certain vows. I was free to follow the Lord wherever He would lead me.

It was such a revelation and liberation to me that I did not come to Jesus because I measured up to other people's expectations, or because I deserved it. I did not have to come to Him as a Bruderhof community member but "just as I am." As this song was sung at my baptism, all my fears of being shunned and "found out" that I was praying with other Christians vanished. I could truly, simply, freely come, just as I am. Being baptized was part of my long journey from bondage to freedom, from needing to obey man's rules and feeling bound to them to being free in Christ to be the person I was created to be. I cannot say enough about the deep work the Lord had to do, and my baptism was perhaps the key experience for me in that.

It was very moving to me that God chose to reach me and show me forgiveness through a Lutheran church. I had learned of the persecution of the Anabaptists by the Lutherans that occurred hundreds of years ago; in fact, the parents of my namesake, little Tanneken, in the *Martyr's Mirror*, were some of them. And now God was teaching me that those times were over, that what happened over four hundred years ago should not separate us now. I had to learn to love, to forgive, and to walk in the new found freedom that I had in the Lord.

John 3:16 has touched millions of Christians all over the world: "For God so loved the world that He gave His only begotten Son, that whoever believes in Him should not perish but have everlasting life." The key part for me is "the world"—that's *everybody* in the world. That doesn't limit God to a given church, mission work, people group, or language. He created this world out of love to have a relationship with Him. His zeal for us was so great that He sent Himself to free us from the bondage of sin, to free us from thinking we are better than other people or that we have the full truth and others don't. I did not know how bound I was to the fear of man and of pleasing man.

When Pastor Yingling and dear Pat quoted this verse to me, I felt so free because I knew that I was a child of God. I no longer needed the approval of others to tell me this. I knew, by faith in Jesus Christ, that God had a destiny for me. I had gone from bondage to freedom and into a true faith walk in Jesus Christ. Even today, as I reflect back on how freeing it was to be washed by the blood of the Lamb, I can only shout "Hallelujah" again.

Now that I was baptized, I knew I was cut off by the community, but my Jesus saw me through it. I felt like I was being carried in His arms, and as if there were a hedge of protection around me. I no longer feared what the community elders might do. My Jesus had led me, and I trusted Him. My faith was still small like a toddler who has to stumble and fall until he finally walks, but I had done it with the help of my dear Jesus.

I felt the separation from my family keenly. As much as I wanted to, I could not force myself on my mother and father, even on the well intended counsel of others. Christmases, birthdays, family events, and national holidays would come and go, but I was not allowed to go home, even before my baptism, and embrace my mother and father. How I missed that.

Around this time, my father became ill. He had been ill for a long time before I found out at a precious family reunion in a state park where I was able to join them. Papa was using a cane, shuffling, and not responding well. I later understood he was suffering from Alzheimer's disease. It was my great desire to be allowed home to serve him and care for him, but even then, I was rarely allowed to visit. However, once he became bedridden, I was allowed to visit him once or twice a month. I thank my mother and my sisters that they let me feed him and sit by his side, though it was difficult for me not to be allowed to help more. I had to learn the loving attitude of Jesus, who asked His Father to forgive those who were crucifying Him. My suffering was nothing compared to what He suffered, and it made my faith ever stronger in Him.

Papa was not responding and usually did not recognize me, but one time, he did say, "Tanneken is here." Knowing that he was aware of my presence gave me great comfort, but towards the end, there was no recognition. As I continued to visit, I knew he was very ill but did not realize how close he was to death. Partly due to my own fears,

I was hesitant to ask too many questions of the community, so I was only called once he died.

I traveled by train for the funeral, and for once nearly the whole family was together. Only my brother Hänsel from Canada was missing, having made his goodbyes to Papa the month before. The same day I arrived, my father was to be buried. As a family, we surrounded the open casket to have our closure with Papa. All was silent. Mama's grief-stricken face was painful to see, and I longed for a comforting word for her and all of us. I asked mother what her favorite Scripture verse was. Thankfully, Mama was able to answer, and John 14:1-3 was read:

> Let not your heart be troubled; you believe in God, believe also in Me. In My Father's house are many mansions; if it were not so, I would have told you. I go to prepare a place for you. And if I go and prepare a place for you, I will come again and receive you to Myself; that where I am, there you may be also.

This comforted all of us. I was allowed to stay for one night and share the communal meal where stories of our dear Papa were shared, but the next day, I had to leave. This felt very hard as I still so needed to be with my family. As I returned to Indiana, I was greeted lovingly by dear Christian friends who comforted me, both in the loss of my father and the rejection I still felt from the community.

Part of my new-found freedom in Christ was learning to forgive. Despite ongoing battles, the bitter feeling, the sting of the pain, would go as I forgave. I learned to forgive even before someone could say "I am sorry." I was like a butterfly coming out of a cocoon learning to fly. I was learning to actually be myself, to find out who God wanted me to be, and not to be controlled by others' expectations. So I forgave and forgave, again and again—and life went on.

Though my life was dedicated to helping the children, I still found their severe disabilities hard at times. It was so heartbreaking! But I remember the Lord speaking to me. "Tanneken, stay with them." I thought of my dear Jesus with the lepers, touching and loving them. These strengthening words from my Lord helped me to do what He called me to do, as I gave a child a cup of water or wiped a runny nose. Pat gave me an acronym to live by—JOY: Jesus, others, and yourself. This became my model. My journey with the Lord was only just beginning. He had so much more to teach me, and so many more ways in which I would be able to serve Him through reaching out to the "least of these."

# Discipled and Called to Israel

*But the Master comes, and the foolish crowd*
*Never can quite understand*
*The worth of a soul and the change that's wrought*
*By the touch of the Master's hand.*
"The Touch of the Master's Hand"
by Myra Brooks Welch, 1921

Despite the wonderful fellowship I had become part of through my friends Pat and Kay, I still yearned for that sense of belonging that my early years in Christian community had given me. My brother Mel told me about a Mennonite fellowship called Fellowship of Hope in Indiana where some members lived in community in a poor area of the city of Elkhart. After visiting, I felt it might be what I was searching for. I was living on minimum wage and had no car so to move was a difficult prospect, but, as with all my years until now, the Lord never forsook me and always provided for me. I moved via rail on the Amtrak service to Indiana, with twenty or thirty boxes of my possessions. At the station, I said goodbye to Pat and Kay, who prayed a prayer of blessing over me. Their love and our pain at parting were very evident, but there was also great expectation as to what God would do in my life.

I joined a household of five and met Lowry and Ruth Mallory, who have continued to pray for me and mentor me until today, and Lois Engelman, a faithful woman of God, now a committed Catholic, who has interceded for me for many, many years. It was Lois who found me crying and reading Psalm 16 after I received a difficult letter from the community. Years later, she reminded me of this, that even then the Bible had become such a comfort to me. In the home, we shared our resources and lived with a common purse, following the early church's example in Acts, and I felt welcomed with open arms into the community and church. We had great times of fellowship together. I

*Maypole dance, May 1, 1984. I (left) was lead teacher for the children of the students at the Mennonite Seminary in Elkhart, Indiana.*

took a post as head teacher in the nursery of the local Bible seminary. I was poorly paid, and I had to use my bicycle for transport, but God was with me, helping me through it.

On Sundays we went to church together as a household, and I witnessed a freedom of worship that was new to me. We sang Scripture songs I had not heard much before; at the Lutheran churches, we had mainly sung hymns. Also, some people even raised their hands as they worshipped. I had never seen that before and really didn't understand it, so I made sure I didn't raise my hands and held my songbook tightly!

This was when I began to learn about the power of the Holy Spirit in our lives. The Fellowship of Hope was part of the Charismatic Movement, and Lowry and Ruth themselves had experienced the baptism in the Holy Spirit. I asked them about it, and finally they told me about a seminar teaching on this subject. With some reluctance but a willingness to learn, I agreed to go.

The leaders took readings from Acts explaining about the Holy Spirit coming down on the apostles at Pentecost where they spoke in other languages and even unknown tongues. Then we went on to look at the gifts of the Spirit (prophecy, healing, the word of knowledge, etc.) in Romans 12 and I Corinthians 12. In particular, I was struck by the words of our Lord Jesus in Luke 11, asking fathers if they would give their children scorpions or snakes when they had asked for fish or an egg. Our Heavenly Father knows how to give good gifts much better than an earthly father! If we ask Him for His Holy Spirit in our lives, He will give Him to us. He won't give us anything that hurts or doesn't edify us in our faith.

When they explained that, I knelt with many others, and they prayed for me for the baptism of the Holy Spirit. I accepted the teaching and the prayer, but nothing happened though I felt happy and peaceful. However, at worship services, I found that now I was able to lift my hands in prayer—you should see me now!

But the Lord had not finished with me yet, and I attended a renewal meeting at a Catholic University. John Wimber from the Vineyard Movement was preaching, and as he preached, there was such a presence of God's Holy Spirit. For me, it was an intimate experience with Jesus Christ Himself. It seemed as if the Holy Spirit was moving around me in peaceful waves, and people were falling down. I had never seen that before, but I just accepted it as part of what God was doing. It was not noisy or disturbing, simply an atmosphere of peace.

I was filled with the Holy Spirit, and I felt myself fully free of all that I had gone through in life, all the strife and disappointments, all the bondage to man's ideas. I worshipped the Lord, praising Him in song, and then suddenly, the gift of tongues was given to me and is still with me today. My friend Lois was waiting for me as the meeting was drawing to a close but saw me worshipping and let me alone. I kept praising the Lord in tongues for a long time; it was like I was in heaven. I can't say I saw a vision, but it was so healing for my own inner life, like a stamp, or a seal—the Holy Spirit's seal—marking the end of a long journey in finding freedom, finding myself, and finding a new living relationship with Jesus.

I so enjoyed being part of the Fellowship of Hope community and church and received much healing there, but again the Holy Spirit was moving me on. It wasn't community life that He was calling me into. I had heard the Gospel on the radio; I was an evangelist in my heart, sharing the Lord with whoever came along, so I wanted to be part of a fellowship that also had this vision.

The community house had closed down, and I had rented a room. On Saturdays, I ate out at a local restaurant, just myself. On one such Saturday, a couple was playing music and began to sing Christian songs. I spoke with them and found out they were studying at the local seminary. They told me about their church, Zion Chapel[2] in Goshen, Indiana, and about their mission work and invited me along. After attending that first Sunday, I felt I had found a church after my own heart.

My first car—"The Ark"—was a 1963 Chevy Bel Air.

Around this time, I bought my first car—a 1963 Chevy Bel Air for $500. "The Ark," which I nicknamed it, served me well and was now my transportation to church.

After some months, I moved to Goshen. Finding myself homeless after a house-share ended badly, I took a live-in post at a Mennonite respite care home for disabled people. Children and adults could come for a weekend or longer, giving them and their families a much needed break. I was very touched by the families, by the tremendous care that they gave, some of them even feeling guilty for bringing their loved ones to me so they could have a break. I would take two or three at a time, sometimes just one, and give them total care—cooking, bathing, and taking them for walks. I was also able to take them to church, and Zion Chapel was so welcoming! It was very important to me to see that these disabled adults and young people were loved by the church.

At the same time, I took part in Project Promise, a ministry to disabled teens and adults. On Saturday mornings, we would do activities, learn from the Bible, and sing songs; we even had a little bell choir. Sometimes people find it difficult to work with disabled people, finding things like drooling discomfiting. But for me, it was fulfilling to care for the "unwanted," following my dear Lord Jesus who touched the leper. One year, we did a Christmas drama at Zion Chapel, with twenty-two disabled teens. One of the boys, Phillip, had learned the soprano recorder, and with much effort, he managed to play a tune in the shepherd's scene. A deaf teenager played the role of a king and signed, "Where is the king of the Jews?" The church was packed, and many of us had tears in our eyes because it was so moving.

For two years, I lived in this home and enjoyed being part of Zion Chapel. Looking back, I can see that the Lord was preparing and equipping me for future service. After not being allowed to use my music for some years in the community, I was now able to develop that gift in my work with disabled children, which was wonderfully freeing for me.

At the Fellowship of Hope, I had been encouraged by the poem "The Touch of the Master's Hand:"

'Twas battered and scarred, and the auctioneer,
Thought it scarcely worth his while
To waste much time on the old violin,
But held it up with a smile,
"What am I bidden, good folks," he cried,
"Who'll start the bidding for me?
A dollar, a dollar;" then, "Two! Only two?
Two dollars, and who'll make it three?
Three dollars, once; three dollars, twice;
Going for three"—But no,
From the room, far back, a grey-haired man
Came forward and picked up the bow;
Then, wiping the dust from the old violin,
And tightening the loose strings,
He played a melody pure and sweet
As a carolling angel sings.

The music ceased, and the auctioneer,
With a voice that was quiet and low,
Said, "What am I bid for the old violin?"
And he held it up with the bow.
"A thousand dollars, and who'll make it two?
Two thousand! And who'll make it three?
Three thousand, once, three thousand, twice,
And going, and gone," said he.
The people cheered, but some of them cried,
"We do not quite understand
What changed its worth." Swift came the reply:
"The touch of a master's hand."

And many a man with life out of tune,
And battered and scarred with sin,
Is auctioned cheap to the thoughtless crowd,
Much like the old violin.
A "mess of pottage," a glass of wine;

A game—and he travels on.
He is "going" once, and "going" twice,
He's "going" and almost "gone."
But the Master comes, and the foolish crowd
Never can quite understand
The worth of a soul and the change that's wrought
By the touch of the Master's hand.

As I was being touched by my Master Jesus, a freedom in following the Lord and worshipping Jesus filled my being. I loved to sing the hymns and Scripture songs. At Zion Chapel, I began to accompany the worship songs with my violin or soprano recorder. This new freedom to play instruments as a love song to Jesus was inspired by songs such as "I Love You, Lord" by Laurie Klein:

I love You Lord, and I lift my voice
To worship You, oh my soul rejoice.
Take joy my King in what You hear,
May it be a sweet, sweet sound in Your ear.

Jesus told me that He is not looking for perfection or great skill but for hearts that worship Him alone in Spirit and in truth. I love to sing to my Jesus in honor and thankfulness for His endless love and good purposes and protection throughout my life. The Holy Spirit led me and brought inner peace and joy to my soul as the gifts God had given me found fulfillment in worship and praise.

Zion Chapel was stretching its wings and becoming involved in short-term missions abroad. I joined them for their first trip to Belize—at that time one of the poorest countries in Central America—supporting an outreach event organized by local missionaries. As a team, we learned how to work together. Some found the tropical climate and basic conditions hard to cope with, but for me, it was very similar to Paraguay (even some of the same birds), so I was a little more used to living with less amenities! I helped lead the children's program, teaching singing, puppets, and crafts; it was a joy to see all the children gathered round, although the poverty was heartbreaking.

I was thrilled to learn anything new that would help me draw near to the Lord, and one new thing was joining a prayer group for Israel. The nation of Israel seemed to have a special pull for me. I had a huge desire to walk where Jesus walked, to cry where Jesus cried, to laugh where Jesus laughed. It seemed like an impossible dream, as

I was still earning only a minimum wage, but nothing is impossible with the Lord. A surprise US tax return was enough for me to travel to Israel with my dear friend Pat and visit the special holy sites of Jesus' ministry on earth. The site believed to be the Garden of Gethsemane was especially powerful as I reflected on how our Lord had suffered there and what He had done for me personally and for the whole world as He died upon that cross and rose again. To be there with Pat, who had been with me through my long struggle from bondage to freedom, was also very special.

This was a wonderful holiday and wrought in me a deep longing to be a bridge of peace to the Jewish people. God spoke to me especially through Isaiah 40:1-2: "'Comfort, yes, comfort My people!' says your God. 'Speak comfort to Jerusalem, and cry out to her, that her warfare is ended, that her iniquity is pardoned; for she has received from the LORD's hand double for all her sins.'"

I felt that God wanted me to be a blessing to His people, the Jews, and that I should go and serve there. I read about Isaiah's call to his people, and his simple answer to the Lord so spoke to me: "Here *am* I! Send me" (Isa. 6:8). Sadly, the Israel prayer group I had joined eventually followed a path away from Jesus that I could not follow, but they had given me some wonderful contacts with Messianic Jews (Jews who believe in Jesus) and the International Christian Embassy in Jerusalem (ICEJ). Through them, I was able to find a post in a Catholic home for disabled children. The Lord was taking me abroad to serve Him and His people. Wherever He led, I gladly followed and was supported by the love and prayers of my church and friends.

## From Ruth Mallory, member of Fellowship of Hope Church and long time friend

The first thought that always comes to mind when I think of Tanneken is how the Lord has had his hand on her throughout her years and how uniquely prepared she is to be involved in her current ministry. When I first met her, it was as part of the Fellowship of Hope, which was a Mennonite intentional community with a common purse for eighteen years. It started with four or five couples who were studying at the Mennonite Seminary here in Elkhart and who wanted a more radical expression of what it means to follow Jesus: simple life style, peace witness and way of life and mutual accountability among the members—with the Sermon on the Mount being basic.

Tanneken came at a time in her life when she was hurting and needed healing; she was searching—she really just drank in all the love and care and sound teaching that enveloped her here. She was such a sincere seeker. Because of her personality, she was a joy to welcome into our household; she came with a lot of knowledge in knowing how to live and share in a common life. She eagerly helped with chores, taking turns cleaning and cooking.

It was a very significant time for her. She had been shunned by her home community, isolated from her family, had been led to the Lord by Christian friends, but she was missing a deep sense of belonging—being part of a community. (After all, she had grown up in a Christian community, which had been a rich experience for her.) After Tanneken became more grounded in her faith and experienced some healing, she searched for a fellowship that was more evangelistic. Can you not just hear her say, "We need to share the love of Jesus!?"

## From Steve Chupp, pastor of Harvest Community Church (formerly Zion Chapel), Goshen, Indiana

When Tanneken Fros joined our church, she made an immediate and wonderful impact. Her passion for Jesus and exuberant personality were contagious. She loves people, especially children and those less fortunate, and is willing to sacrifice a great deal personally to serve them.

Tanneken arrived at our church with a deep passion for Jesus and the church. Her salvation has deep meaning to her. Not only did Jesus forgive her sins, but God made her a member of His family. The local church is where she found genuine love and acceptance, fostering life-giving relationships. To this day, Tanneken is an ardent supporter of our local church and invests fully in those that attend.

It is hard to imagine now that Tanneken once struggled with depression and thoughts of suicide. She knows who her Savior and Deliverer is and lives a life of loving Jesus before others. I often say that Tanneken could give our announcements on Sunday morning and leave people loving Jesus more. All of life is an opportunity to love her Lord and share that love with others.

I have fond memories of Tanneken's first year in our church. Her deep respect for God's presence and for spiritual leadership made an immediate impact on me. Of course, her love and passion for Jesus were also quite evident.

*I thank the Lord for Pastor Steve Chupp, former pastor of Harvest Community Church, Goshen, Indiana, and his wife, Ronda. They faithfully and lovingly encouraged me through 25 years of overseas missions from 1990 through 2015.*

One event that stands out in my mind came in those early days. Tanneken began working with Mennoheim, a residential assistance organization for disabled and handicapped adults. She showed our church how we could love and accept them when she literally carried them to our services. One of the most-attended events we had to that point was the Christmas program she directed exclusively utilizing her handicapped friends. We were humbled and amazed that the incarnation could be so lovingly and joyfully presented by those with obvious physical and mental limitations. Tanneken gave these special people the confidence they needed to perform before such a large crowd.

I was impressed in our first meeting to find that Tanneken is a Kingdom person. While she loved the church, her vision was not limited to a local assembly. She reached outside the church walls to share Jesus. She readily joined our church's mission team to Belize and was a capable and enthusiastic participant. When opportunity came for her to minister in Israel, she assumed this was a natural next step for one devoted to Jesus. We were honored to serve as her home church.

# Jerusalem

*My times are in Your hand.*
Psalm 31:15

The home, called St. Vincent, where I took up my first post in Israel, was in Ein Kerem, a small town near Jerusalem tucked away in a quiet, deep valley. The town is believed to be the home of John the Baptist, where Mary went to visit Elizabeth. Around one hundred children lived in the home, mostly Jewish even though it was run by Catholic nuns. All the children had severe impairments, and some had suffered cruelly. Many volunteers from all over the world worked there, and it was a blessed time for me. I mainly helped with basic care, but whenever there was an opportunity, I would try to include music. Once again, I saw how even non-verbal children could respond and enjoy music and how effective it was as therapy.

I had a great desire to learn Hebrew, for even though Israelis spoke English quite well, many of them only knew the basics, and I thought it would help me relate better to the children. I started going to language classes, joining in with newcomers to Israel from America, England, and many other places. Outside of class, I enjoyed starting to read the New Testament in Hebrew. It was an exciting time to be in Israel, as many Jews were making *aliyah*, the Hebrew word used to refer to the regathering of the Jewish people from all over the world to the land of their forefathers. It was good to get to know people from so many places, and Israel remains a great melting pot of cultures today.

Perhaps the most exciting *aliyah* up to that time was Operation Moses, when over 30 secret flights airlifted 8,000 Jewish Ethiopians, the Beta Israel people, to Israel over a seven-week period in 1984-85. With the end of the Cold War, a wave of Jewish Russians were also coming, sometimes living in great poverty. Though they were supported by the state at a minimal level, many of them still begged for food.

I started to attend a Messianic fellowship, a community of Jewish believers of Yeshua (the Hebrew name for Jesus). We visited many of the Russian newcomers who were often very keen to receive Bibles and Scripture booklets; we also brought them food or something of practical use. By showing the love of God for them, we also showed the love of Yeshua.

*1997: Russian immigrants—professional musicians—played music on the streets of Haifa, Israel to earn a little money.*

As a believer in Jesus in Israel, it can be difficult to share your faith, as there is much opposition from Orthodox rabbis, and people are very cautious about speaking to you. For many Jewish people, it is hard to hear the Gospel of Jesus because of all the persecution they've endured at the hands of Christians over the centuries in the name of Jesus or under the banner of a cross, such as the Crusades. However, because of my German/Dutch background, I was able to make precious friendships with some older German Jews, many who had been through the Holocaust and suffered in such terrible ways. I could talk to them in German, and they would respond in Yiddish; which I could understand a little.

The experience of my parents fleeing the Nazi regime cushioned their feelings towards me as a believer in Jesus and allowed a little more openness. But I was learning too; I was shocked at the horror man is capable of, which I saw at Yad Veshem, the Holocaust museum in Jerusalem. It was especially hard to see such horrid things written in my mother tongue. When I met German Jews, some still with their concentration camp brand on their arm, or the Russian Jews, who had also suffered so much, I could only show them love, love, love.

While in Ein Kerem, I had an accident. I loved to walk in the hills near the home on my days off, and on one such outing, I jumped a small ditch and landed on a stone hidden in the grass. I heard a crunch as my ankle hit the ground. I was alone and in a lot of pain, but I could see the local hospital in the distance, so I started shuffling in that direction. I could not walk. A couple of people helped me; one lady took off her high-heels to get to me and help me to her car. An x-ray showed I had chipped my ankle bone and had to have an operation straightaway.

*1997: I taught music in the therapy program for the mentally and physically disabled at the Swedish Village, Jerusalem.*

*I (right) am celebrating the Feast of Purim with the handicapped children from St. Vincents Children's Home in Jerusalem.*

Still knowing few people in Israel, I felt very alone, and I didn't have medical insurance or a penny to pay for the operation. I was so scared as they prepared me for the operation and put an injection in my back, but the Lord's peace came over me. He gave me Psalm 31:14-15a: "But as for me, I trust in You, O LORD; I say, 'You are my God.' My times are in Your hand." Many times since then, when things in mission were rough, I would sing this verse to myself and feel comforted and secure. As I was hearing the drill put the screws into my ankle, I didn't want to lose an opportunity. I shared with the anaesthetist about God's purposes for Israel; he listened and even commented on King David's life.

I was lonely in the hospital, as I was visited only by the home's social worker; the other staff were too busy with their work. But soon I was back at the home, facing six weeks in a wheelchair. Yet, this led to blessing. It was fun for the children who were able to walk to push the wheelchair and scoot me down the corridors. Since I couldn't do my regular work, I concentrated on using music with the children.

Then the bill came from the hospital—over US $1,000! I spoke with Steve Chupp, the pastor of Zion Chapel, my home church in Indiana, and within a month, the church—mainly the youth I believe—donated enough to pay for the operation. How I thank the Lord for Zion Chapel! They had helped me with my plane ticket to Israel and paid for the printing of Scripture booklets, which, as an evangelist, I enjoy using wherever I go. Now called Harvest Community Church, it is still my home church, and they continue to support my work in missions. It's so important for a missionary to have such a church behind them.

After a year, I moved to a second center, known as the Swedish Village then, home for over two-hundred disabled children, teens, and adults in Jerusalem. Working closely with the speech and occupational therapists, I developed a music therapy program. I put the whole program together in Hebrew, quite a challenge for me as a new learner, and I used many Jewish folk songs, which were biblically based. What a delight that was! Music again proved powerful; the minute you sing or play music to a child who cannot talk, their mind responds and their body starts moving. It was such a precious time.

I returned each year to America for a month or two, and in early 1991, I was on such a break when the first Gulf War broke out after Saddam Hussein invaded Kuwait. As the air offensive began in January, SCUD missiles were fired into Israel, which lasted six weeks. Despite all the uncertainties and danger, I was desperate to get back to Israel, but I took counsel from my church. However, just ten days after the war ended, I returned, renewed in my conviction of God's call and believing He would give me the grace, courage, strength and protection to carry on.

After three years in Israel, I sensed that my work in music therapy was over. I still wanted to continue to bless the Jewish people, but I wanted to be freer to share my faith as I worked. While I was in prayer, I heard God say, "Go north." I had no idea what that meant. Where was "north"? I knew no one in northern Israel. So I just kept praying and continued working where I was, but I knew these words were from the Lord. Sometimes I felt like Abraham, commanded by God to move into unknown territory, but I trusted the Lord, so I waited for Him to show me where He wanted me to be.

David and Karen Davis, a couple who had been involved with the homeless and addicts in New York City with Times Square Church had recently settled in Israel. They had a heart to reach out to drug addicts and alcoholics as David Wilkerson had done years before in the poorest neighborhoods of New York City. I had met them briefly a few times at the Messianic fellowship, but my first significant conversation with Karen was at a worship concert in Jerusalem. During worship, I felt uncomfortable, wondering if it was truly being done in spirit and in truth or more as mere entertainment, so I slipped away and met Karen outside, who was having the same concerns.

This meeting—some would say by chance, but for me, it felt God-ordained—would change the course of my life. As we continued to talk, we found we had such unity of spirit. Karen and David were setting up a project in Haifa—in the very north of Israel! Their goal was to provide a support program for men with backgrounds of drug and alcohol abuse, based solely on the teachings and principles of the Bible. David was himself a transformed alcoholic, who through finding faith had seen his life turn around, and Karen was a Jewish believer with a heart for her own people.[1] They invited me to visit their ministry and told me not to do anything except to pray and see where the Lord would lead.

I visited for a week and observed how David and Karen supported former drug addicts as they left their hard-core street life behind. They did this through prayer and a discipleship program based on the Word of God. I had no experience working with adults so damaged by such lifestyles; all my training was with children. I knew nothing about drugs. I had never knowingly spoken to anyone who had even taken drugs. Yet, the Lord spoke to me very clearly; this was where I was to go to fulfil my calling for Israel. This was where I would obey His word to "Comfort My people," and I trusted Him to equip me for this new ministry. I returned to Jerusalem and resigned from my post at the Swedish Village. Once again, my home church provided support and guidance and prayed for me as I stepped out in faith.

*I am enjoying a camel ride while touring Israel.*

*Sandy (right) and I are visiting the garden tomb in Jerusalem. I shared the Gospel with Sandy who promptly forsook her New Age religion and became a follower of Christ.*

I had loved living in Jerusalem, and spent some time

before I left visiting the sites that were special to me. I returned again to the Garden Tomb, one of two places that is believed to be the site of Jesus' burial. I went to this peaceful, lovely garden with a Danish friend who had worked with me at Ein Kerem, but she was not a believer. At one spot in the garden, you can view a rocky outcropping just outside the garden, which is believed to be Golgotha where Jesus was crucified. While standing there, I read the crucifixion story aloud. Tears rolled down my friend's face, and then she said, "Tanneken, now I believe." It was a powerful moment to see my friend come to faith in the Lord in such a simple way.

I also had to say goodbye to some of the people I had visited with the Messianic fellowship. I remember how sad it was to part with Anna, an elderly Russian Jew, who lived in a single room in a motel. She gave me a beautiful set of Babushka nesting dolls. Anna had not come to faith in Jesus, but I knew that the love we were able to show her and others would have its effect. They may have been just kind words, a little help, or a chocolate bar with a word of God from the Old Testament—all seeds planted in people's hearts. I believe firmly in the words in Isaiah 55:11, "So shall My word be that goes forth from My mouth; It shall not return to Me void, But it shall accomplish what I please, And it shall prosper in the thing for which I sent it." God's Word will not return to Him empty.

Though parting was hard, a new place, a new home, and new friends awaited me. By now, I was in my late forties, and still, as today, a single woman. Perhaps I should say how the Lord has blessed me in this single life. I think back to my early years of childhood, when our family was a healthy unit. It was a peaceful family life aside from the usual sibling squabbles. Despite living in the community, our own family unit was still cherished. Though the community took priority, we were still very conscious of our families. Weddings were celebrated by the whole community; I rarely heard fights among couples or my parents; and I never heard of divorce. So as I grew up, the whole concept of marriage was a very positive one.

During my college years, it was not a problem for me being single as I concentrated so much on my studies. In my mind, I was convinced if I married I would only marry a Bruderhof member. Even during the time working at the day care center in Hartford, I always had in mind I would be going back to the community and then maybe I would marry there. I guess it was not until I returned that second time to the community that a deep desire to be married emerged. I saw my friends marrying, and there were one or two young men who, secretly in my thoughts, I hoped might one day turn their hearts towards me.

In the community, if a young man liked a girl, he spoke first to an elder, and if the elder blessed this, then he spoke to the girl's parents. If they were in agreement, he could get to know the girl, but he had to be a fully baptized member of the community first or it was not even considered. There were very strict rules about touching or holding hands, and it was not until they were engaged that they could sit together at meals. But the weddings themselves were beautiful and included drama, singing, and folk-dancing. Marriage was kept so holy.

When I was a novice, not yet a full member, I was not yet able to marry in the community or even get to know a young man. So I guess the decision to marry or not was not really in my hands in those days. I desired it, yes, but it did not overrule my life. Of course, I had thoughts about what it would be like to have my own child and what my children would be like.

When I was put under church discipline and finally left in 1979, thoughts of marriage were far away. I was more concerned as to how I could put things right, and how I could get back to the community and my family. That was when I was under the bondage of the fear of man, always concerned with trying to please the elders.

Once I became a born-again Christian and the chains of fear were broken, I found my freedom in Christ as a single woman, and being single was not a burden to me. Pat was a very good example to me. As a single woman at that time, she had fully dedicated herself to helping the disabled and underprivileged, and I learned from her in this. I was learning who God created me to be, to be a unique, distinct individual, not conforming to another's mold. I began to find completeness in Jesus.

In Israel, in my forties, for the first time, I joined a singles group at an international Christian fellowship based in Jerusalem. I had never felt a need for this before. I had kinship with others who were also single and was living a full life, serving my Lord through serving His people. I was suspicious of singles groups, thinking they were more about finding a partner, but I found that it was not like that. The group leaders, Reuven and Yanit Ross, had the great gift of encouragement and would quote Corrie Ten Boom, "Don't be so preoccupied with who you aren't."

Of course I desired to get married, but this desire never paralyzed me; it never stopped me from moving forward. If that desire dictates our lives, we miss out on what God has for us in our singleness. It is a gift to be single and a gift to be married,[2] so I'll make the most of my singleness. My life today continues to be fulfilling as a single woman of God. I continue to build my relationship with God, and worship is especially important to me because that's when I feel the love of God the most. What is important is that we always fix our eyes upon Jesus, whether single or married, and that we first seek the Kingdom of God, knowing that all else will follow. This is not a pat answer, but it works for me!

I thank the Lord that He has helped me in this, and that I can still do what He wants me to do—working among orphans and widows and churches in my beloved African home—even though I'm single and now in my sixties.

## From Karen Davis, co-founder of Beit Nitzachon, the House of Victory rehabilitation center, and worship leader at Kehilat Carmel, an indigenous Messianic congregation

I remember a significant event when mine and Tanneken's paths crossed that showed me a lot about Tanneken. A Messianic music group had come to Jerusalem for a concert. I was there and I was grieved by what I was hearing. As a worship leader, I'm sensitive to the difference between performance and entertainment versus real worship to God, real ministry to God. I actually walked out, and who did I run into but Tanneken, who had walked out for the same reason. It seemed like everyone in the auditorium was so happy and enjoying the concert, but I felt grieved in my spirit and so was she. That may have been our first really significant conversation. I saw such a love of God in her that was so completely unworldly; that was the beginning for me of seeing that this lady had quite a discernment in the Spirit. We felt a real connection in the Spirit. We stayed in touch with Tanneken, and she had a sense that we were to work together, and so we invited her to come up and be part of the work that we were doing.

# House of Victory, Haifa

*Adonai ori v'yishi, mimi ira?*
*The LORD is my light and salvation, whom shall I fear?*
Psalm 27:1

(Some names and personal details have been changed in this chapter.)

I traveled to Haifa by public bus with just a few suitcases of clothes and moved into the upper floor of Beit Nitzachon, the House of Victory. David and Karen Davis had rented this property for their support work with those with backgrounds of drug and alcohol abuse. It was built into the lower northern slopes of Mount Carmel, as is most of Haifa, with a beautiful view over the Mediterranean Sea.

For my first year there, my main responsibility was the kitchen. We would have up to ten people at a time in the home, usually men. Any women lived upstairs with me, and so I became involved in counseling the women, learning as much as I could from colleagues. People from both Jewish and Arab backgrounds came to Beit Nitzachon, which was very unusual for Israel. But David and Karen believed very strongly in working towards reconciliation between the two, and we saw many people from both backgrounds live together and go through the program successfully.

Those who have come from backgrounds of drug and alcohol abuse often have very poor diets and even suffer from malnutrition. Some we worked with had been living on the streets, stealing anything they could to sell for drugs. My home cooking was an important part of their recovery, and the kitchen was a favorite place for everybody. One or two of the residents helped me, which in turn helped in their rehabilitation. We tried to cook healthy, balanced meals, and I learned to make Israeli foods: pitas filled with salad and hummus and topped with lamb or chicken. My special dish was good old apple pie; oh how they loved that! It was wonderful to see the change in people just from eating regular nutritious meals. The residents very quickly gained weight, and step by step, we saw them restored physically, underpinning their mental, social, emotional, and spiritual recovery.

The House of Victory program placed people in a protected setting, but, of course, temptations were very great. We had strict rules; even smoking cigarettes was not allowed. It was not for everybody though. Some managed only two or three days before leaving, but others came through totally delivered from drugs and living a life of witness and love as a believer of Jesus.

*1994: A wedding at Kehilat Ha Maschiach, a Messianic congregation in Jerusalem. Friends of mine—Russian immigrants—were married under the Kupa.*

One of the first to live with me was a girl called Maria, who was pregnant and living in very poor conditions. I was asked if she could live with me until the baby was born. She was a dear girl, who became a believer in Jesus. We had wonderful Bible studies and prayer, and she helped me around the home. For a time, I guess I was like a mother to her. Eventually, she married her boyfriend, who had been through a similar program in New York City and was helping at House of Victory. She asked me to be the mother-of-honor, as she came from a country where the mother is the maid-of-honor.

I went to the hairdresser, and for the first time in my life of nearly fifty years, I wore make-up and had my hair done! The beautician did a gorgeous job, and the wedding was beautiful. I have lost touch with Maria and am not sure where life has taken her, but I pray that the time of restoration in Haifa has borne fruit for her in God's eternal kingdom.

Susanna was a tough cookie, disillusioned with life and addicted to drugs. She arrived bandaged up with a slash in her arm she had received in a fight. She was with us many months and step by step received healing from all her woundedness and disappointments. She began to help me in the kitchen, but she worked so slowly, I had to be very patient with her. When she went back home, she continued to fellowship with Messianic believers. Months later, I heard that she chose to go to a Bible school and that she was doing well.

Daniel was a Jewish man, who from early in his life had grown up in a children's home. Stealing became part of his life from an early age, and as an adult, his was a life of theft, especially cars. Addiction to cigarettes, drugs, and alcohol followed. He came to us in his late forties or early fifties, nearly blind, probably because of substance abuse.

*I am playing my violin at a celebration at House of Victory which houses a rehabilitation program for those addicted to drugs.*

The day started at Beit Nitzachon with personal prayer time and Bible study groups and then a time of practical work. Daniel took part in this routine, but because of his poor vision, he helped me in the kitchen rather than on the grounds. He found purpose in this, and we had opportunity to talk. As time went on, he showed me his notebook, where in big letters and few words, he was starting to learn the Word of God. Daniel finished the program victoriously and returned to his home town, where I believe he serves the poor through a local ministry.

One young man, Yariv, who was using drugs and involved in the New Age movement, which was very strong in Israel at the time, came to us saying, "I hear you help people." He became a devout believer, preaching the gospel fearlessly, even though speaking out could lead to much opposition. We held many beach outreaches in Haifa and found many who were hungry to hear of God's love, especially those from the former Soviet Union.

*Me (left) on my 50th birthday with Karen Davis (lower right)*

Kehilat HaCarmel, or Carmel Assembly— the congregation led by David and Karen on the same property with Beit Nitzachon—was in its infancy in those days. We met on Shabbat, the Jewish Sabbath that begins on Friday night and ends on Saturday night. I became part of the worship team with Karen Davis, playing my violin. I felt I shared in a revival of true worship at this fellowship, learning many of the Hebrew songs and seeing gifts of music, song-writing, and prophetic proclamation at work in their worship times.

*Menorah banner used in the celebration of the biblical feasts*

As I continued to study the Scriptures on baptism I felt the Lord showing me that I should be immersed in water. So, simply out of obedience to God's Word in Romans 6:3-4, I was baptized by immersion in the Mediterranean Sea by Peter Tsukahira, one of the pastors of Carmel Assembly. Some may say this was not necessary since I had already been baptized, but for me to be fully immersed beautifully pictured what had happened to me spiritually (see Colossians 2:12) and brought a sense of completeness.

Celebrating "the feasts of the Lord" (Lev. 23:2) in Israel with the Jewish people as part of Kehilat HaCarmel was a wonderful experience that has shaped my Christian practice until today. In September-October, all over Israel during the Feast of Tabernacles, people build themselves shelters and sleep outside, looking up at the stars and remembering God's protection over the people of Israel during their forty years of wandering in the desert.

At Hannukah, or the Festival of Lights, in December, the Jews remember the rescue of the Jewish people in the second century BC and the miracle of oil. When the desecrated Temple was restored, the golden candelabra only had enough oil for one day but burned for eight. Messianic Jews remember Yeshua, the light of the world. But most special was the Passover celebrations, so meaningful for Jewish believers who understand the fulfillment of this Passover meal in our Messiah.

Within the congregation, I also helped with Shabbat school, teaching and encouraging the children. I now see how everything that I experienced in my years in Israel was a preparation for what the Lord was leading me to. I always have encouraged myself with the certainty that God never asks us to do something that He himself does not equip us to do through the leading and power of the Holy Spirit.

After a couple of years it became difficult to have men and women being treated on the same property, and I could only take on one woman at a time in my upstairs apartment. We began to pray for a new property just for women. After much prayer and intercession, we found a new place which we called Beit Ha Tikva, the House of Hope. My home church, Zion Chapel, took a step of faith in supporting this, providing for the rent and my food, which before I had not had to pay for.

I became the coordinator for the women's ministry and began taking in women with very damaged backgrounds along with my co-worker Renee. I saw perhaps eight women come and live with us, each with a different story. By the grace of God, some were fully delivered from their afflictions, but for others, who were not quite yet ready to leave their damaging lifestyles, perhaps we were just part of their journey to freedom.

I still had so much to learn, so it was a great blessing when Yanit and Reuven Ross, who had run the singles ministry in Jerusalem, moved to Haifa. This couple had—and still have—a heart for pastoral care, and Yanit helped me in learning to disciple these women. She

*In 1995 I was privileged to march with the nations gathered in Jerusalem to bless Israel during the Feast of Tabernacles.*

came up to help offer counselling to them, and I would often sit in on her sessions with the women, learning all I could and helping her in prayer ministry. We worked with women facing many different difficulties, not just from drug abuse, but some who were battling with self abuse or eating disorders. We had to be so patient and deal with lots of lying. You couldn't jump all over them and accuse them, but you had to help them face up to what they had done, so that they could get free.

Chana came to live with us from a terribly wrecked life of prostitution, of many partners and of drug abuse. I remember showing her the Jesus film while she was going through withdrawal, a very

## He who dwells in the secret place of the Most High

Tanneken Fros                                          Haifa, Israel 1995

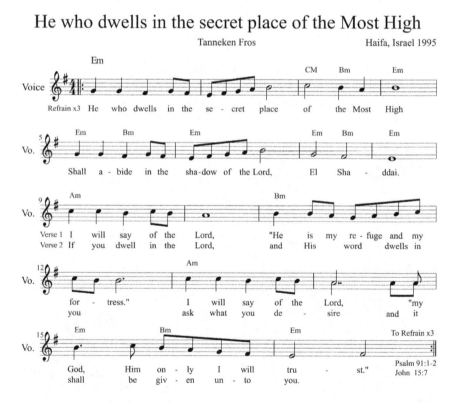

*This is a song God gave me as I was ministering to the hurting women at House of Victory, Haifa, Israel. I have sung it many times since, especially in difficult times when I needed to trust the Lord as my Refuge and Fortress.*

painful process. Even though she was groaning with pain, she was listening. Suddenly, she asked me about John the Baptist.

"Isn't he the one that baptized for the forgiveness of sins?"

"Yes," I replied, "but Yeshua forgives."

"Ah, now I understand," was her response.

A tiny seed had been planted. One of the first nights that Chana spent in my apartment brought her to the realization how different life can be away from the streets. At the breakfast table, she said, "Thank you, Tanneken. It is the first time that I have slept in a clean bed in over six years." Yet, Chana argued with me over our rules, especially the cigarette rule. One day, I found her smoking tea leaves wrapped in toilet paper; she was that desperate. She chose not to stay with us and, sadly, returned to her life of drug abuse. I invited her back many times, but it was not to be. You cannot override a person's free will. I can only pray that the seeds we planted will be watered by our Father in Heaven.

During my five precious years in Israel, I was able to witness its ongoing restoration as prophesied in the Word of God, "'For behold, the days are coming,' says the LORD, 'that I will bring back from captivity My people Israel and Judah,' says the LORD. 'And I will cause them to return to the land that I gave to their fathers, and they shall possess it'"(Jer. 30:3). Jews from 103 nations were returning to the land of their forefathers in great numbers. Isaiah 35:1-2 talks about the desert blossoming upon their return, and I witnessed the greening of the desert with the ingenious agricultural systems that truly made the desert bloom. They also planted great forests of pine trees to bring the rains in. Thousands of tourists came from the nations to bless Israel and to help with this reforestation.

There are now many thousands of Messianic Jews. At Kehilat Carmel, it is their deep desire to be reconciled to Arab Israelis, and, we saw Jewish and Arab believers worshipping side by side, as "one new man" (Eph. 2:11-16), Jew and Gentile together. In Romans 9-11, the Word of God says that Jewish people remain God's chosen people, and that they are the apple of His eye (Deut. 32:9; Zech. 2:8). All believers in Jesus who aren't Jewish are "grafted in" like wild olive branches into a cultivated olive tree (Rom. 11:16-24). I have learned not to take sides on the Palestinian issue or involve myself in the politics. God has a solution for the conflict there; I can only pray and try to understand God's side. I loved Israel; it had become my home, and I saw myself serving there for many years, perhaps the rest of my life. Our Father in Heaven was about to reveal a totally unexpected path.

## From David Davis, founder and senior pastor of Kehilat Carmel and co-founder of Beit Nitzachon

When I think back to some of the women that came through our ministry, if I told you about their lives, your hair would stand on end; you name it and they had been into it. Men had tortured one woman—put cigarettes out on her body; she had burns all over her body, and she was addicted to heroin. Tanneken was one of the major forces in not giving up on women like that, that the world would say was totally hopeless.

That's not to say she didn't get exhausted. It's just exhausting working with people with life-controlling problems that have been into such degradation with such demonic forces at work. It's exhausting; it's 24-7; it's around the clock and Tanneken wouldn't give up—that's the tenacious part about her. She had faith and hope for anybody, even though most people thought you could never help that person. Tanneken never felt that way. But she never equivocated; when a woman had a problem, she would deal with the sin issue, but she would do it with such love. She would not skirt the issue, enabling them to stay in their habits that were destroying them. She counseled with the Bible, with the Word of God.

## From Joy Greig
## colleague and friend at Kehilat Carmel

I think she didn't judge people. It would apply to someone who had come off the street and looked a mess or didn't smell very nice or said the wrong things and swore...language you know she'd never heard anywhere...it didn't seem to turn her head at all. But it would also apply to a teenage girl in the congregation who was maybe going through a bit of a thing and dressing a bit weird, and everyone was not quite sure how to talk to her...Tanneken would just go down the middle and talk...

## More from Karen Davis

Our next door neighbors at the time that Tanneken was here were an elderly German couple who were Holocaust survivors. The husband was dying of emphysema. Our little worship group was having rehearsals in our apartment, and Tanneken was part of that team with her violin. This man would come over, because he just loved being around the worship. Tanneken visited him, partly because she spoke German, and when he got really ill, dying in the hospital, she was one of the last people to visit him. I know that she spoke very openly with him about the Lord. The Lord was really using her in all kinds of ways here.

Tanneken was here during the early years of our congregation being born, and she was our first Shabbat school teacher; she ran the children's ministry. We prefer to celebrate and express our faith in the Messiah Yeshua (Jesus in Hebrew) through the Jewish biblical holidays, such as Hanukkah rather than Christmas, and to build bridges of understanding to our Jewish people. I remember Tanneken preparing a special program with the children for Hanukkah. She taught them a song, "Adonai Ori," which means "The Lord is my light," and she had the kids coming in with candles, and it was so beautiful. Her love for children was so clear from the beginning...

# Where is Mozambique?

*Pure and undefiled religion before God and the Father is*
*this: to visit orphans and widows in their trouble ...*
James 1:27a

Since finding the Lord, wherever I have traveled, the church has always been my family, and Zion Chapel, now Harvest Community Church, has been that for me since 1985. They have not only supported me with prayer and encouragement when gone on mission, but wonderfully welcomed me on my return visits as well.

Before I returned for a home visit in 1997, our pastor, Steve Chupp, wrote and asked me if I would like to receive prophetic ministry from Keith Hazell. I was a little hesitant over this, but I knew Keith, a visiting minister who has been so important to our network of churches, and knew he based everything on the Word of God. So, I fasted and prayed in preparation, and then with many others, received prophecy and prayer. Keith, along with Clem Ferris, now a leader in my church, prayed and spent time listening to God on my behalf. This is part of what was prophesied by Keith:

> It's almost like you wear blinkers. You can't look to the right or to the left. You have your eye on one thing, and the thing you have your eye on is the thing that totally consumes you. You are like a finger pointing—that's what the Lord has shown me—you are like a finger pointing at its object and objective, and the Lord is using you to point things to people who have a heart and mind to seek that which you have fixed yourself on.
>
> You are a woman which has had a very interesting experience. You have been many places in many spaces and seen many faces, hallelujah. You are one of those people who is spiritually ambidextrous; you can do two things at once; you can do it with either hand. The Scripture says whatever

your hand finds to do, do it with all your might. This is what you've always done. You've done things that nobody else would do; you've done things that nobody else wanted to do; and you've done things that other people should have done. There's just an incredible thing about you, about being the one that stands in the gap. You can almost change your appearance on occasions, so that you fit the situation. There is something about you that is uniquely pliable; there is something about you that fits in.

You spend time, I think, often living in other people's houses. You spend your time as part of somebody else's family. You're kind of a suitcase believer, hallelujah. You carry most everything that is valuable in your case, and you travel light, hallelujah. You are a person that is at home in different cultures; you are one who is a representative...an ambassador is the word that I get for you. You are one that is sent out as a representative, even into the nations. You have such a vision for the nations that you find yourself in different places, sometimes with extraordinary people...

...You and the Lord have a very interesting relationship, hallelujah. I think you say things to God that the rest of us wouldn't dare to say. You have a directness of approach to the throne of God. You don't play around with things that get in between. You have a heart of intercession in you; you have a heart of caring—there's a tremendous caring. You have a tremendous care for people's needs, almost like a nurse; you've got that same nursing spirit, nurturing spirit. I see people who are deprived, just turning towards you. I see you with a big bag full of toys walking amongst children and just passing them out, and children being attracted to you like bees round a honey pot. You have a unique charisma of your own.

I see that the Lord opens doors for you, almost literally. I see you passing over borders that you're not supposed to pass over. Hallelujah. You're part of God's underground; you sort of have your own tunnel underneath borders from time to time that you travel through, and when you arrive in another country, people are surprised to find you there. Sometimes, it's almost seems, sister, like you've been transported; you suddenly find yourself there—the customs man looks at you, and instead of throwing you out, he lets you in, and he doesn't even look at your passport, hallelujah.

Sister, God says that there is an opening of the opportunity that you have been hanging on to for several years. For several years, you have been...you have been pressing the Lord for one particular door that would open. God, this one, this one. And God opened another one, and you said, "Fine, but what about this one?" You've been [through] some fine doors, but not through this door yet. And the Lord says that He will open an effective door for you, even into that place that has been on your heart and on your spirit.

God says that there are days ahead of you when you will have a greater sense of team than you've sometimes had in the past. There's been a loneliness, sister, because not many people wanted to go where you've gone and the way you've gone. They haven't really had the intestinal fortitude to do that. There hasn't really been in them a desire to take risks. You're a risk-taking woman; you're a woman of faith and woman of confidence...

...Sister, there's a great power in your hand. God says there's a healing anointing in your hand. God says He wants to release this healing anointing. I see you laying hands on little children. I see you laying hands on old women and old men, on whom everyone else has given up. I see you in hovels and shacks, laying hands on people that everybody else has forgotten. You've got a heart quite like Mother Teresa's in that sense. You just embrace the poor, embrace the needy, and God says healing will flow from your hands, and even the Lord says to you there is an extension of life for you because of the healing in your hands.

I believe that the Lord has already told you that he is extending your life; you will have more years, even more years than you have had [in the] past in your family. You will be one that lives beyond the family age, because God has purpose for you into the next century, into what is happening. Sister, you're going to raise up some young people around you that are going to be so fervent that they will frighten the other young people that they meet. You're just going to catch them with your vision, and when you catch them with your vision, you're going to capture them for the Kingdom of God. Sister, lots of anointing, lots of appointing. I think you have a great fun life, hallelujah...

Clem also spoke, comparing my life to an unfinished totem pole, something that stands as a visual legacy, something for people to see. He saw my life being chronicled for other's inspiration, not written by me but by someone going alongside me. I would never have dreamed that my little life story would be put into a book.

Of course prophecy needs to be weighed very carefully and needs confirmation. I was given time with Steve Chupp to talk through its meaning for me. Psalm 37 has been a great comfort to me throughout the years of my Christian life, especially verse four: "Delight yourself also in the Lord, and He shall give you the desires of your heart." For others perhaps this would be to get married, to go on a journey; I don't know what, but for me, the deepest desire of my heart was to serve the Lord by caring for orphans. Perhaps this was the door that Keith felt I had been knocking on for years.

This desire has its roots in the witness of the Bruderhof community. Knowing that they had fled the Nazis, I remember hearing that they took in Jewish children that were orphans, and that touched me and left an imprint in my heart that it was important to care for orphans. I had no idea then that the Bible says that—it was just human compassion. I found out later that James instructed the early church on this: "Pure and undefiled religion before God and the Father is this: to visit orphans and widows in their trouble, and to keep oneself unspotted from the world" (James 1:27).

From early on in my walk with Jesus, I felt impelled by this simple command. I had been very struck by the witness of George Müller, who through prayer and faith had built up a large orphan work over 150 years ago in England.[1] Through my work in America and Israel, I had cared for orphans at times, although most of the disabled children and adults I had worked with came from loving families. While still in Massachusetts in my first job with disabled children, I even considered fostering one of the young people, but it was not the right time. I was probably still too inexperienced in life.

God had been preparing my heart for a different task. In Israel, especially when caring for such severely disabled children, I came to recognise that deep desire within me to be a mother to them, to care for them, to mother, to love—a desire that is in each woman—a love that could be expressed with orphan children who could not be cared for in their own homes.

In our team prayer meetings in Israel, we would regularly pray for the work of Iris Ministries, founded by Rolland and Heidi Baker in Mozambique. They were just beginning their work in those early 1990s in a country emerging from decades of civil war, and they had faced much difficulty and persecution. Their first children's center was shut down by the government, their property confiscated, the children left homeless. Yet, they were seeing God work in miraculous ways, even in the multiplication of food in the most desperate of times. I thought of their ministry as one that cared for orphans, but going there never entered my mind.

Shortly after I received the prophecy, I was given the gift of a holiday by a blessed couple, Mervyn and Anna-Mary Shrock. They were like an adopted father and mother to me, caring for me practically and spiritually. They became family for me when I still felt cut off from my own family. I accompanied them for a week to a retreat center, a wonderful time of hiking, canoe trips, worship, and time alone. During the retreat, we went to see a children's choir from an orphanage in West Africa, who traveled the world each year to perform and fundraise. They sang African folk songs, planting and harvest songs, and songs about our Lord. I listened with tears rolling down my cheeks, and I heard the Lord say, "Go to Mozambique and bring worship to the children." I turned to Anna-Mary and told her what the Lord had said, and then asked, "Where is Mozambique?"

I experienced the Lord's healing on that retreat. I was suffering badly from hip arthritis and the pains were severe. The minister one evening called out those who wanted prayer. I didn't go forward but extended my hand in prayer for others. Yet, as we were praying, I felt a hot wave going through my abdomen and touching my hip like an electrical heat wave. The pain went away and never returned.

I still didn't quite make the link between the prophecy and this word from God to go to Mozambique. Yet, God kept speaking. Mordecai's words to Esther, "Yet who knows whether you have come to the kingdom for such a time as this?" (Esther 4:14) came clearly to me. I began to see that everything I had experienced, all that God had taught me, was in preparation for what was now to come.

The impact of following this call began to dawn on me: "Oh, this means leaving Israel." I so loved being in Israel and in fellowship with my Arab-Israeli and Jewish brothers and sisters! I cannot say it was an easy thing to leave a land that was so dear to me and go again to another land that I knew nothing about where I knew no one. But I knew the children would be orphans—the deepest desire of my heart was being birthed.

How would I tell David and Karen, my beloved colleagues in Haifa? I was coordinator of the women's program, volunteers also stayed with me, and I was so involved in our Carmel Assembly, helping in worship and with the children. It was a lot to leave behind.

On my return to Israel, I asked to speak with David and Karen over a meal. I was hesitant, feeling we had just started the women's ministry. Even though it had been two years; it was only beginning to bear fruit, and we had just opened a separate home for women. So it was with apology that I shared with them the call to Mozambique. But God had gone before me.

While away in New York, David had seen a video at Times Square Church of a team going out to Mozambique. He felt clearly that God was telling him to release me to go to Mozambique to work with Iris Ministries. He and Karen kept this to themselves until I spoke with them. It was such a confirmation of God's call and a great relief to me that I had their support! They felt God had spoken this way to help ease my own feelings of letting them down by leaving. We have a God who cares about all aspects of our lives.

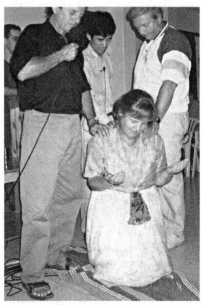

I wrote to Zion Chapel, who responded very positively. Rolland and Heidi Baker had replied to my application to them, saying I was very welcome to join them and would be free to develop the work of worship, drama, arts and crafts, and discipleship with the children.

Within weeks, I had closed up House of Hope, putting some of my things in storage and giving many, many things away. I didn't hold onto anything in particular,

*September 1997, from left: Pastors of Carmel Assembly in Haifa, Israel—David, Peter and Reuven—pray for me as I am being sent into mission work in Maputo, Mozambique to help Rolland and Heidi Baker, Iris Ministries.*

knowing that God had moved me on. I packed two big suitcases with a few clothes and things that I thought would be useful with the children. My dear friend, Yanit, who had previously lived in South Africa, was able to help me prepare for some of the differences in life I might experience. God has used her in so many ways to advise and mentor me.

I received a great farewell from Israel—a really loving, family farewell, one that I will never forget. The congregation had prepared a feast for me, and I was sent out as the first "messenger" of the fellowship of Mount Carmel to go and minister in another land. They have continued to support me with prayer and with gifts, and to this day, have an active part in the ministry to orphans in Mozambique. As I left Israel, Kehilat HaCarmel were building their new worship center right on the top of Mount Carmel, the very place where Elijah called down fire on the prophets of Baal. Even today, more than fifteen years later, most of the ministry in the congregation is run by people who were once addicted to drugs or alcohol and have come through the program at Beit Nitzachon.

Six weeks from my return to Israel, I found myself boarding a plane in Tel Aviv, bound for Maputo, the capital of Mozambique. I was going to find out just where that country was.

*I (center) am at the Tel Aviv Airport in 1997, obeying God's call to go to Mozambique.*

# Iris Ministries

*Who shall not fear You, O Lord, and glorify Your name?*
*For You alone are holy. For all nations shall come*
*and worship before You, for Your judgments*
*have been manifested.*
Revelation 15:4

I arrived at Maputo airport very tired after a 10-hour flight. It was small and dusty with mosquitoes flying about, and right away I became very aware of the risk of malaria. I had informed Rolland and Heidi Baker of my arrival time, but there was no one at the airport to meet me. I waited. Hours went by and no one came. I began to panic. I had no way of contacting the center by phone because all our communication had been by email. I prayed to the Lord, "Please send someone." I sat there with my two suitcases worrying about theft. In all my travels alone, I had never felt as vulnerable as this.

The airport was about to close, and I began to think, "What on earth should I do?" I ordered a taxi, deciding I would need to find a motel. At the last possible moment, two young people arrived. Rolland and Heidi had left for a conference and had given instructions to pick me up. So great was my relief, I almost fell into the arms of those young people! Everything was fine.

I was taken by truck to Rolland and Heidi's apartment and was warmly welcomed. All the confusion over picking me up was cleared up, and I thanked God that He had safely brought me to the place He had called me to. I would first be living in a missionary house in Matola on the outskirts of Maputo, and after a couple of days of rest and orientation, I would be taken to the tent village of Machava.

After eviction from their first orphanage, Rolland and Heidi Baker were left with over 300 orphans to care for and nowhere to house them. It was one of their darkest hours and yet one where they saw

God meeting their every need, sometimes in miraculous ways.[1] They were given the use of land and then army tents to house the orphans. This was Machava, where I began my support of their ministry to very needy young people.

It was quite an experience to drive along the bumpy dirt roads, weaving in and out of homes made from mud and sticks and then through vast fields planted with cashew trees. Often we passed warning signs for landmines. I was now in a land that had seen years and years of conflict. The war against the Portuguese colonial power and the subsequent civil war left millions of landmines over the whole country, and the area around Maputo was especially affected. We could never walk anywhere where there was not a path or a road. Many local people were killed or maimed by these brutal devices. I thank God that many areas of Mozambique are now cleared of mines, but in some areas, even twenty years since the fighting stopped, the danger still exists.

The half-hour ride became my daily routine with my fellow missionaries in an old truck we nicknamed Lazarus—for all the times it had broken down and then come back to life! Each child Iris Ministries cared for had their own story of sorrow or abandonment. Inside the army tents, sometimes there were beds, and other times only simple reed mats, as is common there. Conditions were difficult.

Machava was very sandy, and it was hard to keep things clean. Water had to be carried from a well a 10-minute walk away; this was hot and heavy work. What a joy it was when a well was finally dug on our grounds! Classes and activities took place in simple buildings with metal roofs and reed walls, and they would get very hot as the day wore on. The rainy season was a trial; keeping the children dry in their tents during heavy rain was always a problem. The fields around Machava had not yet been cleared of landmines, so we constantly reminded the children to stay away from them, but there was always the fear, "Will I get hit by a landmine?" It meant that playtime was not as free for the children nor for us who watched over them. We never had any such accidents, but we met a neighbor whose foot had been blown off by such a mine.

There was much for someone from a richer nation to get used to, and perhaps my childhood in Paraguay helped me a little, but the children coped with grace and cheerfulness. They gathered to pray before a simple breakfast of a roll and tea or a bowl of chima—mashed corn—before going to school in the mornings, which was on site in one of the reed huts. Lunch and the evening meal would be rice or massa—boiled cornmeal, usually with beans or maybe a little fish or vegetables.

The afternoons were for activities, and this was when I began to have craft and music sessions, anything I felt would stimulate and encourage the children. Heidi and Rolland were gracious in allowing me freedom to develop this ministry. We did drama and told Bible stories. Having few materials, I had to be inventive and would stock up on supplies on occasional trips to South Africa. Finally, I had found the place where I could fulfill my long-held desire to work with orphans, and as the months went on, I longed to also live with them.

Portuguese was commonly spoken, but in those early days I began to speak to the children in Spanish, which I had learned from my childhood in Paraguay and is similar to Portuguese. The children laughed, saying I spoke "portospañol." I guess I created a new language! With time and practice, my Portuguese improved. Shangaan was the local language in that part of Mozambique, but I only learned a few phrases such as "Canimambo Xcuembo Xamatimbah," meaning "Thank you; God is great!"

Encouraging the children in worship was one of my greatest joys. I gave recorder lessons and taught the older children who wanted to be part of the worship team. During a retreat back in America, I thought and prayed about God's call to me to bring worship to the children, and He brought Revelation 5:9 to my mind: "And they sang a new song, saying: 'You are worthy to take the scroll, and to open its seals; for You were slain, and have redeemed us to God by Your blood out of every tribe and tongue and people and nation.'"

When the children sang in Shangaan, there was such liveliness, even fire, in their singing. I understood that God had called me to enable these children to worship but not in a language or style that was foreign to them. My role was to equip them, to support them in expressing their love for Jesus in their African way. I felt very strongly that I, together with Mozambicans and especially the children, must enter into Mozambican worship. I believe that revival flows from true worship, and over my years here, I have seen this many times. When I think of those words from Revelation, I am reminded of how important worship is and that whatever revival may follow has to come with Mozambican expression.

Worship was so central to our ministry. Heidi and Rolland purchased a circus tent for our church, which was very much a children's church with a lot of dancing and singing. I encouraged some of the older ones in learning guitar, and of course, there was drumming. Dust flew everywhere, coming up from the dirt floor. I was seeing the start of revival, revival out of the dust, and it began with the children. I had not heard children pray as much before, but these Mozambican children prayed, preached, and danced with all their might.

I had brought a shofar, a ram's horn, from Israel. In the Bible it was blown when going to war or to gather the people together, and for me it was also a reminder to pray for peace in Israel and for God's purposes to be completed in Israel. During one time of worship, I blew the shofar and proclaimed a word of repentance. One of our teenagers, Norberto, fell to the dust in the Spirit. Heidi asked me to pray with him. He was quiet in the Lord's presence, and then he started praying and weeping before the Lord, "Lord, help me to read and write."

About 13, Norberto, through various circumstances, had never had the capacity or privilege to learn to read and write. I remember the children gathering around him to pray for him. One little child, David, who was no more than six years old, laid his hands on Norberto and prayed for him. Norberto ended up being Rolland and Heidi's right hand man as far as leading praise and worship with the children, even

*Pastor Rego (standing center) is praying at a revival meeting in Doa, Tete where there was a severe drought. The two men sitting to his right are the chief and his assistant who received the Word of the Lord and were saved. After intense prayer for one hour, rain fell. There was great rejoicing that day!*

preaching, and in later years, I remember him studying in the upper grades of high school.

The Bocaria, the city dump, was one of Heidi's favorite places where she would go "treasure hunting." She introduced me to her friends who lived in this fly-infested, filth-ridden place with not a speck of water to be had. Abandoned children often scavenged for any scrap they could find. It soon became one of my favorite places too as I joined in our weekly trips there. We'd sing with them or just sit and visit with them. Despite the conditions, we felt the peace of God—and we *did* find treasures!

Arsenio had lived in the dump for a long time, abandoned by his parents who had gone to South Africa. He always helped us to translate and to distribute food. He was six years old when he came to live with us. I don't know how many baths I gave him before all the dirt was truly gone. New treasures like Arsenio came to us all the time, and Rolland and Heidi did not turn them away. The Lord had spoken to Heidi very powerfully as she tells in her book, *Always Enough*, through a vision of Christ giving her a piece of His body that multiplied in her hands. He told her that there would always be enough because He had died. This vision gave me and all the team such encouragement

*1999: I am on a mission trip with Mozambican pastors, traveling by canoe on the dangerous, crocodile-infested Zambesia River to a remote church in Malawi. I am seated in the back end of the canoe.*

because there were days when we didn't know where the food would come from. But God was faithful to His Word. We never went hungry, and there was always enough.

Street outreach was not always easy, and sometimes dangerous, with even the authorities acting towards us with hostility. I once took a group of young people on a short-term mission to minister in word and song and to give out soup and bread. Suddenly, a police car pulled up, addressing me as the leader, telling us to get out as we had no permission to do this outreach. I tried respectfully to inform him we did indeed have permission, but he was not convinced, and I and some of the older boys had to go to the police station to be interrogated. They let us go, warning us not to do it again. Well, we cannot bind God's Word, so we gained another permit and continued to go out weekly. We were not detained again.

I met Helena on such an outreach. Her story is told by Heidi and Rolland in their book, *Always Enough*. She had lost a leg and used a crutch to come see us. She came to live with us, and she was always a friend to me. I tried to have a little time with her as often as I could. Finally, one of our South African friends gave her an artificial leg, which was a great help to her, although hot in the summer. She was another treasure, just waiting to be found, for whom the love and care of Christ made such a difference.

Machava was becoming very full, and with only metal-roofed buildings, it was a very hot place to live and work for most of the year. This in part contributed to my first major illness in Mozambique—a severe kidney infection, probably due to dehydration and my malaria medication. I ended up in the hospital for two days. Thanks to Jesus I recovered and, in general, despite catching malaria at times, I have remained healthy and able to cope with the heat over the years, again perhaps due to my childhood in the tropics of Paraguay. Eventually cinder block buildings were erected, which were better able to shelter us from the heat, but there were not enough to house all the needy children whom Rolland and Heidi would not turn away. By faith they kept believing that there would always be enough for one more.

During my first couple of years with Iris Ministries, Rolland and Heidi purchased another parcel of land near Maputo for another orphanage. This would become Zimpeto, and as building began and foundations were laid, we sometimes took the children around the property to pray for it and anoint it. It was marvelous to see the work being built up in this way, and even today both properties are being mightily used in the care of orphans within Iris Ministries.

The missionary house I was living in was closed, so some of us moved to Zimpeto to help start Iris's new work, which then became the center of their ministry for many years. We moved there as the first children moved in with only a reed fence dividing our missionary compound from the youngest children's home. We could hear them crying in the morning during their cold baths. But living on the grounds with the children made us all feel more like a family. They were allowed to come in and out of our home when we invited them, and we could pop over any time, be it in the evening to sing goodnight songs or say goodnight prayers with them. During this time I also helped Heidi coordinate the children's daily program.

This marked a new phase in the work of Iris Ministries. Rolland and Heidi felt very strongly that they needed to tithe the first building at Zimpeto to be a Bible school for local pastors. This would enable them to learn more of the Word of God and to encourage them to do church planting and discipleship in their communities. However, there were very few Bibles available to local people then. In some remote places, pastors would perhaps only have a tract to preach from. The first 12 students arrived, mostly from central Mozambique, and the Bible School began, right in the center of the orphan work. Early in the morning, we could hear the pastors praying together for God's will to be done and for their families they had left behind for these months of training.

Alongside our Mozambican brothers, Rolland and Heidi had begun their preaching and church planting ministry, going further into the country to encourage pastors and churches way out in the bush. Our Lord's great commission to us in Matthew 28:18-19 had always struck me with great power from my early days as a Christian. Jesus' first words in these verses, "All authority has been given to Me in heaven and on earth," gave me great comfort, knowing that God is in control. Now, in my first years in Mozambique, I felt this great urge, like a fire burning within me, to go on these mission trips to share the gospel of Christ.

My first trip was in central Mozambique, an 18-hour drive to the province of Sofala, where we were taken to a very remote area. Two pastors, Pastor Tomo and Pastor Rego, wanted to accompany us, but since it was difficult for us to say exactly when we would arrive, they waited for two days by the side of the road! When we finally met up, they were dusty, tired, and hungry, having had nothing to eat all that time.

The village they led us to was in the bush, remote and isolated. We had to leave the truck and walk along a path deep into the forest. Through the trees we saw a group of people sitting on benches made of branches. This was their church. There was no building, just a clearing in the forest. As we arrived they got up and danced with joy. We joined them on those stick benches, ignoring the discomfort. Everything is worthwhile when the Gospel is preached.

I admit I was a little uncomfortable going so deep into the bush on this first mission trip. As my fellow missionary Brian started preaching, a large, green, very poisonous snake fell from a tree right in front of the altar. At first fear overcame the people, but it didn't last, and that snake was soon dealt with. Many were saved that day; it was worth it all.

Jesus left everything to come down to this earth. He left His Father and the glory of Heaven to walk where you and I walk, to suffer what we suffer, and to be with the poor, the prostitute, the injured and disabled, and the murderer. He did not have His own house or bed, but because of His love for us, He did all this, and then He died for you and me. Every time I went through hardships in the mission field, the Lord reminded me that He came for such as these. My part is to simply show the love, mercy, and compassion of God and share His Gospel of salvation wherever I go. My own hardships were as nothing compared to what many people of Mozambique had to face daily just to survive.

On another trip we traveled inland to a place called Manica, again way out in the countryside. The church we were visiting was made of mud, and people were sitting on benches made of sticks. As we arrived, Heidi asked me to preach. This was a new thing for me; I had never really preached before in this way. I faltered, telling Heidi I hadn't prepared, but she insisted, "No, you can do it; just pray and preach today." I stepped outside the church and prayed, and the story of blind Bartimaeus came to me, where Jesus asked him, "What do you want Me to do for you?" (Mark 10:51). I was able to preach, telling the gathered congregation that Jesus was asking them the same question.

As I talked, I felt God speaking to me, telling me to call forward one of the elderly ladies in the front row. One stepped forward. Aida was blind, but I did not know this until she was in front of me. She had big white cataracts on her eyes. She had seen in years past, but now she saw

*I am preaching in Salinhanga Tete, a remote church located far from civilization, where leopards roam. What an experience to enter this village at night and then to praise the Lord and preach the Word! Jesus met the assembly in a wonderful way!*

*Children gather around me during a mission journey in a remote area of Chimmanimani, Mozambique.*

nothing. Faith welled up in me, and I mixed dirt and spittle and put it on her eyes. Heidi and Pastor Joni came and laid their hands upon her and prayed. This lady was very gently slain in the Spirit, overcome as it were by His power. We continued to pray that she would be healed, and Aida opened her eyes. The white cataracts had totally disappeared like a blanket had been taken off, and I could see her beautiful brown African eyes. Aida saw! God had done a miracle. It was the first miracle I had seen with my own eyes. I have met Aida since, and years later we heard she was still in her fields, sowing her corn, planting her seeds, reaping her harvest, and caring for her family.[2]

The meeting went on with the Holy Spirit working in great power, with people even being set free from demon possession. One woman admitted hating her husband and her whole family. As we talked with her about the power of forgiveness, a great peace came over her. God was teaching me He can use anyone, even me, when I feel out of place and unprepared. As the new millennium began, I needed to rely on God more and more, for Mozambique was about to face perhaps its greatest catastrophe.

# The Floods of 2000 and 2001

*The war was nothing compared to this. During the war*
*you could run away from the enemy. But the water*
*affected everyone and left us with no refuge.*
From *Mozambique and the Great Flood of 2000*[1]

For many Mozambicans, flooding is an annual worry. Mozambique is low lying, and rivers run through it from the central highlands of South Africa and Zimbabwe. Every year in summer, the heat and humidity rise and torrential rains follow. Rivers such as the Limpopo and the Zambesia break their normal boundaries and run out into the floodplains, sometimes for miles. This is life in Mozambique; often roads and homes are flooded, and great difficulty is caused, but it is something that is known and understood as part of the cycle of the year.

The floods of 2000 were not like this. Four floods over three months caused unprecedented destruction and suffering. At its peak in late February, an area almost the size of my father's home country, the Netherlands, was underwater, and over 500,000 people were made homeless. Many people drowned. Mozambique hit the world headlines with pictures of people clinging to trees and huddled on roofs. A mother gave birth to a baby girl whilst clinging to a tree. Their dramatic rescue by helicopter was filmed, and this helped create a massive international response.

In Maputo, it was in early February that the worst devastation occurred. Cyclone Connie blew in from the Indian Ocean and almost 18 inches of rain fell on the city's airport in just two days.[2] The floods did not reach us at Zimpeto, but we were very worried about Machava, which was on a lower plain. A message came through from José and Raquel, the missionaries running Machava, that it was totally flooded. Nearly two hundred children and staff had to evacuate on foot, and we needed to get to them.

Every truck we had was mobilized. On one of my visits back home, my dear church back home had given me funding for a four-wheel-drive vehicle, and just before the floods arrived, I had purchased an Isuzu. So I set out with my colleagues, driving through up to two feet of flood water. Whole roads had been washed away. All around us people were struggling to rescue their belongings, carrying chairs and pots and pans on their heads, trying to reach the safety of higher ground.

We worked our way slowly through, but we could not reach Machava. In fact, as we came out of Maputo, the road had become a river. My truck was pushed by the water, and I was afraid of being taken right off the road. We cried out to the Lord for protection. We just wanted to rescue our orphans who we knew were suffering in this flood, just like all the people around us. The Lord encouraged me again with His words in Isaiah: "When you pass through the waters, I will be with you; and through the rivers, they shall not overflow you" (43:2). With God's grace, I was able to steady the wheel and pass through.

José and Raquel were leading the children on a journey to Zimpeto that took over half an hour by car in good conditions. Some of the small ones had to be carried; they were all exhausted and soaked to the skin. Finally we met them on the road. What a reunion that was! We piled them into our trucks and turned around to go back through the waters, knowing God was with us.

Our home in Zimpeto was not too affected by the floods. Machava, however, was so badly damaged that the children could not return there for some time. The dining room alone was in flood water a meter deep, so the children stayed in Zimpeto. We squeezed them in wherever we could, as Heidi loved to say, "There's always room for one more." Almost daily a new child arrived; so great was the need during

*2000: With the help of Mozambican pastors, I am wading through the flood waters in Maputo. We distributed World Missionary Press scripture booklets, drinking water and bread to thousands of flood victims*

*One of thousands of mud huts destroyed in the flood of 2000 in Maputo, Mozambique. The family still lives here.*

the floods. In all, we were caring for around five hundred children.

In Maputo as a whole, thousands of homes were flooded. It was usual then for people's homes to be made of reeds in the south of the country, so everything was ripped and crushed. The rushing waters turned roads into impassable ravines, making any form of travel really difficult. Clean drinking water was scarce; malaria and cholera increased. Yet we saw people returning to their flooded properties, hanging things up and reclaiming their homes. Many of our own children and staff contracted malaria, but we were grateful that no cases of cholera were found.

Many thousands were left completely homeless. They had to live for some weeks in accommodation centers set up by the government. One center was in a vacant cashew factory. Six thousand people crowded into that place, each family having just a reed mat, maybe a pot or pan or a few clothes, and some with nothing. The government started food distributions, but was overwhelmed with the size of the task. Other nations and aid groups helped, but because of difficulties with transport, the food was often delayed. Sometimes people would tell us they hadn't eaten for two or three days. With students from our new Bible school I began to visit the cashew factory, bringing what supplies we could as supporters gave to Iris Ministries and preaching the Word of God.

It seemed humanly impossible to make much of a difference. People may wonder what difference our work made in the face of such enormous need. What difference does it make to bring just a loaf of bread? Dear ones, we must do what we can. Stop for the one. Listen to the one. Pray for the one. Bring a loaf of bread for the one, and one more little soul will be comforted. One more little soul will have hope. As we preached the Word of God in those camps, people would burst

*A church in Villa Doze, one of many churches planted following the 2001 flood in the province of Sofala at the center of Mozambique*

into singing and dancing. They expressed such joy over the fact that someone had dared to visit them in their misery.

We had no Bibles to give, but World Missionary Press had provided us many Scripture booklets printed in Portuguese and also in local languages. I remember one family, a father with his children huddled around him on their reed mat. When I gave him the booklet, "Help from Above," tears rolled from his eyes as he said thank you. To know that just one person was so encouraged in the midst of such severe circumstances was great encouragement to me.

Whenever we could, we brought food and supplies. Though people would thank us for the food, it was Bibles they wanted the most. Instead of asking for bread that would meet their immediate physical need, they were crying out for the Word of God, the true Bread of Life. One accommodation center was previously a warehouse during the communist regime. Marxist pictures and slogans were written all over the walls. As I got ready to preach the good news of Jesus and His salvation, I noticed that the words "Viva Marxism" were written all over the walls. The Lord spoke to me and said, "Turn it around and have the people proclaim, 'Jesus viva' (Jesus lives)." In one chorus, the crowd proclaimed many times, "Jesus viva." In the midst of such catastrophe, the nation was being born again.

As the weeks went on, areas north of Maputo were devastated by further flooding. A huge refugee camp grew around the main road in Chókwè, about a hundred miles north. It was a city of tents with sixty thousand people. We decided to take a truck load of clothing, food, and Bibles. As we drove there, it started pouring with rain. The ground was so saturated that it could easily have prevented us from getting through. We prayed together that the rain would stop, and as we approached the camp, the rains started to ease. By the time we arrived, it had stopped. We were able to deliver the supplies to the camp's distribution center, and the rain held off while we gave out Bibles and boxes of Scripture booklets to the community leaders. Just as we had finished, the rains started again.

In another area, some villages were completely cut off, and only helicopters were able to bring in supplies. I went with Heidi and a group of our pastors from the Bible school to see what help we could bring. We had to wade waist-deep for over an hour through the floods, which were very dangerous—you never knew if there might be snakes or crocodiles nearby! We prayed for protection as we carried water containers, food supplies, and Scripture booklets on our heads through the waters. Crowds of hundreds of people were waiting for us. Some food had gotten through to them but not enough. We could not bring much, just a little bit of everything, but I believed that every sign of love and hope would encourage many. They received the Word of God in our booklets with gladness—indeed it was hard to keep order as we handed them out!

Mount Sushi in Murrumbala, Zambesia. During the civil war from 1972 to 1992, a miracle happened at this mountain. Angels (there is no other explanation) pushed open the approximately 20-meter-high slab of rock. As people entered they received a plate of food. When they had finished eating they had to leave. Today, this enormous rock portal remains closed. Only white doves are seen flying in and out of the crevice.

Day after day, we continued to bring whatever we could to the victims of this terrible flooding, many of whom were not able to return to or rebuild their homes for many weeks. People were so generous in their giving, and Rolland and Heidi worked alongside many other Christian organizations and the government to help as many as possible. It seemed too great a task, yet we relied on Jesus, walking in His presence and guidance. We prayed we would do just what He had planned for that day.

The people at Zimpeto, the missionaries from around the world, the local staff, and, of course, the children, all had become my family. As a single woman, I have always appreciated that the people I am alongside in ministry and the people I am

2002: While on a mission trip to do a conference with Iris Ministries, I got to hold one of my namesakes—a little Tanneken.

ministering to become my family. Special events such as birthdays or Christmas are not times to be away from them on a little holiday. The best place to be is to be with them. Possibly the separation of over twenty years from my own family prepared my heart to be family especially to the orphans. Of course, I wanted to be with my mother and father at Christmas, but as this was not possible, I really made the most of wherever I was. However, just as in Israel, when I seemed to be finally putting down roots, God was calling me on.

I had visited Pastor Rego and his dear wife, Cecilia, in the small town of Dondo in the center of Mozambique, but I did not know much about them or their ministry. We sat outside his mud-built home on a rickety bench in the shade of a mango tree, and he shared the call he felt to care for orphans. As I listened, my heart began to stir. I had originally met him at Zimpeto as one of the first of our Bible school students. I had noticed he appeared to make time for the orphans, talking and playing with them when he was not studying.

A little while later, I accompanied Heidi to a conference in Manica Province near the Zimbabwe border. At the hotel before the conference began, both Heidi and I were together, but separately in prayer for the meeting ahead. I felt the Lord say that He was sending me to the center of the country to work alongside Pastor and Mama Rego. I sat quietly and waited for Heidi. She came out of her prayer time and said she felt it was the time to fortify and strengthen the churches in the center. Before I had spoken of the Lord's word to me, she asked if I would be

2005: I am visiting one of the remote MOP churches in Zambesia and am holding another Tanneken, one of my 11 namesakes in Mozambique and Malawi. I am being gifted with a chicken by little Tanneken's mother.

willing to move to this area and assist the development of this new phase for Iris Ministries.

The Lord greatly blessed that conference, and we were able to pray for hundreds of people. As the meeting came to a close, a little old man came and knelt next to me. So I knelt down next to him, and he said he wanted to receive sight. He had only blurry vision. I laid my hands on his eyes and started praying, asking the Lord to clear his eyes. Then I asked, "Any better?" He replied, "Not yet." So I laid my hands again and continued to pray. He opened his eyes, and the miracle occurred. He jumped up and ran up to the stage and said that the Lord had restored his vision. Hallelujah!

On returning to Zimpeto, I spent time with Rolland and Heidi, and they both supported me in this new calling, feeling it was the Lord's will. I thank the Lord for my home church, Zion Chapel, who so faithfully supported me through all this change. I shared with them this new calling, my concerns at having no place to stay, and knowing no one in that area except Pastor and Mama Rego. They simply encouraged me to look at what the possibilities were and get back to them.

So in late 2000, I moved to Beira, a city in the center of Sofala Province, just a few miles from Dondo where Pastor Rego lived. It was very sad to say goodbye to the precious children of Zimpeto, who by now called me Tia Tanneken or Aunt Tanneken. For four months, I rented a room at the Beach House, a Christian guest house, overlooking the sea. Each morning, I would see local fishermen setting out in canoes made from hollowed-out logs. It was a beautiful setting. But my heart was to live in the community served by Pastor Rego and to see how I could help develop their orphan care.

Psalm 68 speaks very powerfully of God's heart for the orphan: "A father of the fatherless, a defender of widows, is God in His holy habitation. God sets the solitary in families" (vv. 5-6a). This very much influenced my thinking over orphan care. God created us to grow up in families. Zimpeto and Machava were wonderful places where each child was loved and cherished, but that was hard for local people to do on a smaller scale.

Iris Ministries began to develop a program from Zimpeto to help care for orphans within families. Along with Pastor and Mama Rego, I hoped to develop church-based family orphan care to see how local churches could be encouraged to reach out to the most vulnerable children in their communities. Pastor and Mama Rego took in ten orphans, and this grew within months to nineteen.

A little mud-hut extension was built for me on the side of their home, and I moved from Beira to fully support the local church in this new ministry. Heidi and Rolland asked me to oversee the development of their ministry in the central and northern areas of Mozambique, and I was helped by Darryl Greig, who I had also known in Israel.

The following year, further flooding caused great suffering for many in Mozambique, hitting the center of the country the most. In many ways, these floods were as devastating as those in 2000, but the response for aid was much less. We visited accommodation centers, bringing food when we could and offering prayer and Scripture booklets.

Rolland and Heidi sent support and came themselves on outreach trips. Darryl organized much of this, always going out with the flood teams. Our own orphans came with us at times and helped with praying and encouraging people in those centers who had lost everything and were suffering greatly. Our children, so much in need themselves, learned to have compassion on those who were worse off than they were.

## From Darryl Greig, fellow missionary currently serving with his family in Nampula, Mozambique

I moved to Beira in early 2001. The Bakers thought I would be a good support to Tanneken. I didn't always find it that easy; I didn't always find her approach to things were what I would do. You see, Tanneken had this enormous area of responsibility; she was basically looking after Iris's work in the north of the country, and there was a lot going on. I got sent out organizing conferences, organizing a bunch of people arriving from the States to places where there's not even electricity. I think that they were things that would have distracted Tanneken from the things that were most strongly on her heart.

I wound up doing flood relief when the Zambesia was flooding. I worked with a guy from Jesus Alive, a South African organization. It was very different to the Maputo floods; there wasn't the money coming in, and there were very few resources for Iris Ministries. The people up there are poorer, they've got less access to stuff, and they are more ignored. There weren't very many camps, a few along the river, but there were a lot of people displaced by those floods. It wasn't dramatic; it was a slow-rising flood, but it was devastating. The Zambesia, to a certain extent, floods every year, but it was a bad flood; there was a lot of area under water.

Then of course the crops didn't plant, and so there was famine, especially in Malawi; people got hungry then. People were eating the leaves off the trees and the grass off the ground. I think Rolland called me up and said, "What are we going to do about the famine in Malawi?" I'm just so full of faith that I said, "Nothing, what do you mean? There's just me." He said, "We have to do something. These are our churches up there; we need to care for these people." He asked Pastor Surpresa to travel with me. Pastor Surpresa is an astonishing man of faith, and the Iris Ministries national director; he arrived with some resources to try and help.

With Tanneken, I remember we were going somewhere, and Tanneken had done something with the key, and that entailed me leaving her wherever we were and driving a decent drive back to find the key. I, in my gracious way, went muttering...and somewhere on the way God met me, met my heart, and said, "This is what you're here to do." I remember laughing out loud in the car, and thinking, yeah, this is what it's all about.

I got the key and came back, and I found Tanneken had spent the entire time preaching to whoever she could get her hands on, wherever I had left her, in the bush somewhere. She was just preaching to those people, and I thought this is why people like this are so effective. There are no dead times for Tanneken. Every time, every situation, was an opportunity to say, "What is the Father doing now, and how can I join in?" I found that tremendously challenging.

Rolland said this several times. We'd be traveling somewhere and either Tanneken or Heidi would have made some administrative blunder or made some impossible plans, and he'd say, "But these ladies, they see milked-over, blind eyes healed." Maybe that's what it takes to see milked-over blind eyes healed. They just pushed forward, and they got on with it. When it came to detail, Tanneken did get flustered, but the enormity of the task didn't ever seem to overwhelm her.

# Dondo Becomes Home

*Takulandilani! Landirani Mzimu Woyera.*
*Welcome! Receive the Holy Spirit.*

Iris Ministries was seeing a huge growth in church planting in the center of Mozambique, and we began to consider setting up a more permanent home for the ministry. Heidi and Rolland found a beautiful orchard for sale in Dondo. We felt the Lord working in overcoming difficulties as this land was purchased, and we hoped we would see a church, a clinic and a Bible school built there among the trees. Experienced local pastors were brought together to help teach and disciple others, and the Bible School began. Students would come for three months each year when it wasn't farming season.

I had a special burden to do evangelism and took the students out each Friday to do outreach in the communities. At the same time, I worked on the food distribution to widows and orphans, but my heart's desire remained the work with orphans. I hoped to start sharing a home of my own with orphans. I moved out of Pastor Rego's house and rented a property for myself and other missionaries and visitors, whoever was serving with us at the time. Zion Chapel, my home church, helped me with this, again, always providing for whatever the Lord called me to do.

In those early months in Dondo, there was of course many difficulties, but we saw the Lord at work in powerful ways. One Sunday, Pastor Rego, Cecelia, and I went to a church for blind people and their families, and he preached the gospel of salvation. After that, I preached on the wonderful invitation of Jesus to His marriage feast for all who accepted His invitation (Luke 14:16-23). People came forward and publicly confessed their sins including teenagers. What a revival the Lord gave that day!

The following Sunday, they came to our church in Dondo. We saw, I believe, a glimpse of heaven as these dear families and others joined us for a wonderful worship service, followed by a "feast" of goat meat, chicken, rice, vegetables, and juice, served by our children and the widows we supported. I just sat back for a moment and thought: "Thank you, Jesus, for allowing us to see a glimpse of how it will be in heaven at this great marriage feast. Lord, You are fulfilling Your Word of this marriage feast where the blind, the lame, and the poor never reject Your invitation, and here they are being served by orphans and widows." This day is deeply implanted in my heart; I will never forget it.

I then began to develop a relationship with the school for blind children in the city of Beira. In those days, the school's conditions were very poor, particularly for boarding children. I asked the director if they had any orphans, and he introduced me to Joana. Just about six years old, she sat in a corner, dirty and pale. She was too nervous to be touched or hugged, a very closed-up little girl. Her parents had died, and her uncle had brought her to the school, promising to visit, but he never did. When the school was closed for holidays, she had to stay at the children's hospital because she had no relatives who would keep her.

It was agreed Joana could stay with us for weekends and vacations, and she was one of the first orphans to live with me. Over the years, she has grown and flourished and has become a dear little friend. She is a lead singer in our orphans' choir. She has a good memory and loves to tell Bible stories. She was told at school she could not learn Braille because of some problems with her fingers. I felt the school needed to think a little wider and asked them just to try and teach her, and now she is finally learning.

She has started to move up the grades after years of repeating the same class. She has friends in her classes and now sometimes chooses to stay at the school on weekends but returns to us for holidays. Joana is loved by the children in Dondo and has a special relationship with the widow who also shares my home. She discovered faith in Jesus, and after she confessed her faith, it was a great joy to see her baptized with other believers at one of our Christmas services in a pond among the rice fields.

"Treasure hunting" with Heidi in the rubbish dump of Maputo had very much affected my heart, so we began to visit the local dump in Beira every week, holding little church services and bringing soup and bread. We found various children there digging for scraps. Sometimes they would come and live with us or be found a home with one of the church families. I also got to know the children begging in the city center as I went about my errands; often they were helping disabled relatives to beg. There was no state support for ill or disabled people and no opportunity to work. Begging was a way of helping to provide for themselves and their families.

Manuel was about 17 when I met him. His uncle was blind and unable to walk, so Manuel carried him into town, helping him to beg for money. Every time I went into Beira, I would chat with him and give him a little something; this turned out to be a real friendship. One of his relatives, Lino, came to live with us when he was about 10. He struggled at first, and we worked hard with Manuel's family to support him properly.

Manuel's family were themselves living in utter poverty, hardly a roof over the shack they called home. They became involved in our church, and Manuel later married. They moved to live near Pastor Rego's home in the rice fields of Dondo and lived a better life, going on to have two daughters. Sadly Manuel has since died, but through his support, his uncle, Senhor Costa, with his wife who is also blind, has joined and remained part of Pastor Rego's Mountain of Praise church. He and his wife have just dedicated their fourth child to the Lord.

Lino moved to where another relative lived in Beira, our neighboring city, when he was about 16. He is participating in another church and I believe is one of the youth worship leaders. Lino is an excellent worship leader and teaches worship teams. He often visits us, always encouraging our children to worship and dance.

My new rental home was a blessing, but living further away from Pastor Rego and the church had its dangers. Yet the Lord's hand of protection was with me. On one occasion, I had traveled with Pastor Rego and some other pastors on a small mission trip further into Mozambique. We had another trip planned right afterwards, but had planned to return to Dondo in between. I sensed that we didn't need to go back to Dondo and shared this with Pastor Rego. So we stayed the night as guests of our fellow believers.

That night there was a horrific robbery at my home. My two guards were attacked; one was bound and blindfolded, and the other was badly beaten and threatened with a knife. The robbers crashed down my door and ransacked my home for two hours. They stole our projector, a new laptop that my home church had just given, as well as money and many other things. My bedroom was turned upside down.

I believe it was the Lord's providence that I was not there. My dearest friend Jesus had protected me from this horrific experience, and miraculously my guards were not seriously hurt. Of course, when I returned and entered my home, I wept. I had never seen something like this; my home was completely trashed. It seemed like Satan wanted to stop the work of the Lord. Fear did not stop me though. I continued to live there, but improved the building's safety by putting up security bars. Rolland quickly responded and gave me a computer. Bit by bit things were restored but never the projector we had used so many times to show the *Jesus* film.

Rolland and Heidi's ministry was growing and growing, reaching across borders. Many churches in neighboring Malawi were being founded. With Rolland and Heidi, I had the opportunity of going to many places to preach the gospel, and everywhere we went, we were welcomed very warmly. At our first conference in Malawi, over a thousand people gathered. We were seeing revival, people kneeling on the dusty ground and coming to repentance, revival out of the dust.

At every meeting, we saw such a sweep of the Holy Spirit. Heidi preached on James in the sweltering sun with sweat just dripping down. She invited people to the altar, and many came running, falling onto the ground and crying out to the Lord for revival for themselves and for Malawi. Heidi prayed for them to receive the Holy Spirit, and the gift of tongues was given to many hundreds. It was like a sea of tongues. I had never experienced anything like that. It wasn't a big glorious fanfare, but there was glorious change, glorious worship in the utmost of poverty.

The Lord has encouraged me through dreams and visions many times. When I was still in Israel, I dreamt of a huge rainbow, its colors clear and bold, its lower edges on fire, with flames leaping up. At the time, it encouraged me to think of the awesomeness of God, of His promises, and of being purified through the fire of trials and tribulations. It was such a clear vision that it stayed with me over the years.

In 2003, Heidi and Rolland organized another conference in Malawi. This time 10,000 people came from all over the country. It was a "Fresh Fire" conference, and I felt the Lord reminding me of the rainbow vision, so I painted it on a large banner that hung over the stage, writing underneath, "Welcome, receive the Holy Spirit" in Chichewa, the language of Malawi. It was such a blessed time, with

*2002: As I was preaching the Gospel in a remote area in the district of Dondo, everyone, including the chief, raised their hands to receive Jesus as Savior and Lord of their lives.*

many saved and filled with the Holy Spirit. But the real miracle for me was the order among the people as we served out food for so many. People were so patient; our two hired guards were also amazed. It felt as if we had a host of angels with us. I was so conscious of our team of twelve intercessors—and of course of my faithful home church—praying throughout the whole conference. God was in this and only the Lord may be glorified. Hallelujah!

We saw the Lord at work at our Dondo Bible School property also and were privileged to see Him work in miraculous healings. We saw children speak who previously could not. But the Lord does not always answer our prayers as we imagine. Daniel came to live with Pastor Rego after his elderly grandmother could no longer care for him. She lived in very poor conditions herself, and her health was failing. Daniel had become profoundly deaf, after being able to hear as a young child. Neither could he speak. When he first came to us, although he was already nine years old, he did not have a name, and so I called him Daniel. He settled with us, and I brought him along to one of our conferences.

Heidi was with us for that conference, and we soaked Daniel in prayer all evening, praying that God would open his ears and mouth. He was not healed that night, but the next day he began to speak, his first word to me being "Jesus." From that day, he could speak in Masena, the language of his family, and I would see him conversing with Pastor Rego and others, much more able to join in with our church family life. Daniel's deafness continued, however, so we continue to pray and trust that the Lord has His hand on dear Daniel. Now, Daniel goes daily to the only existing deaf school in Mozambique. He is in 5th grade and is doing well.[1] He converses quite well with me in Portuguese. Daniel loves the Lord. It is a touching scene to see him in church with his Bible and one of our youth interpreting for him what is being preached.

Iris Ministries was so special to me. Rolland and Heidi had trained me in mission. I was privileged to work alongside them as a sister in many situations. I was with them when we witnessed healings, at the food distributions, and among the children. I truly enjoyed developing the children's program of crafts, music, drama, Scripture memory and having Rolland and Heidi's full support in it. It was most meaningful to me to be asked to teach on evangelism and worship in their Bible school. I learned from them, always looking to the Lord and trying to do what we could in the face of unimaginable need. Yet change was coming that would see me stepping out on my own in partnership with my Mozambican brothers and sisters.

## From Antonio Boisse, a student

In 2001, I was ten years old. I lived with my grandmother. She was very sick while I was living with her and later died. Where we lived there was no secondary school. The municipality came where I was living with my grandmother and said that I had to come to her [municipality] office so we can discuss this. When I came to the municipality offices in Dondo, they took me to the Social Services office and then they took me to the mission ministry for orphans.

There is a mountain of things to tell of how the mission has helped me. First of all, they gave me a place to live, and they then started paying for my education. Through being part of them, I became a Christian, and in Mozambique, it is written in the law that each child has a right to religion. By coming here and with getting to know Mama Tanneken, I really became integrated into the ministry. I have personally experienced a great change. Before I had this help, when I lived with my grandmother, it was in great poverty. I managed up to fifth grade in school, but I never dreamed that I would continue. Now I am in eleventh

2010: Mountain of Praise church youth choir directed by Boisse, one of the orphans who grew up in the church's orphan care program.

grade. [Antonio has since graduated from high school and hopes to enter medical school one day to be a doctor.]

The first day I came to the mission, Tanneken came there in the evening. I was talking with other children and when Tanneken arrived, she asked me, "Who are you? What's your name?" So I gave my name and Tanneken said, "Come, let's all clap hands for him." I remember especially when Tanneken left for mission journeys; Mama Tanneken always remembered to buy something sweet for the children when she returned. She never forgot to speak to us about the Word of God. Mama never forgot to encourage us with the Word until today, and I never forget it because it helped me so much.

Just a few days ago, I was thinking what name can we give Tanneken, and I thought of "A mai dos encoragamentos," the mother of encouragement. In our culture, any lady with Tanneken's age, we would call her Mama as the polite way to speak to her. But in another way, our Mama here, she shows all the love that a mother shows, and that's why it just sticks for us. She is our "Mama." Mama helps everybody, and I believe this gift that Mama has is a divine gift that has been given to her. Wherever help is needed, Mama helps.

## From Caetano, a student

I have lived here since 2001. Before, I lived with my older sister; we were three brothers, and she herself had her own children, three daughters. She was not married, and she couldn't manage to also care for us, and so she asked if we could live here [at the orphan ministry]. At first, I lived in Pastor Rego's home. Tanneken came, bringing toys one morning. We had breakfast together and then we started playing with these toys. She was very creative in playing with the children, so we always played together, and there was much joy that day.

I am in tenth grade, and I would like to be an architect. Tanneken encouraged me to be an artist and they have printed cards I have drawn. I [am] also learning to become a "Levite" [a worshipper]. I remember one day we went to a mission in Beira, and in a seminar, we learned about how to worship God. This was good; I liked it very much, and I liked the encouragement it gave me. This has helped me until today to worship God.

I am beginning to help others and am involved with the children. I like very much to teach them the way to God. Sometimes I stumble over things. Mama Tanneken helps me, she counsels me, and she helps me onto a good path. I pray and hope God helps her. She has also helped me in a practical way to play the guitar. I play the guitar at church, and I like that very much. God is opening more doors for me and for Tanneken too.

## Joana, a student

I have two brothers but I do not know where they are. I lived with my uncle. My uncle came to drop me off at the institute [Beira's school for visually impaired children]. He promised to visit me, but he never came. During the holidays, I would have to go to the children's hospital because I had no other place to go to. I got to know Mama in 2003. I was glad that I could go home with Mama Tanneken. She gave me clothes, she helped me to study, and she helped me to learn English. She plays with me and helps me to learn to tell Bible stories. Mama encourages me to sing. I am now a lead singer. I hope to learn to translate Portuguese to English. [In English] Good night, Jesus loves you!

# New Beginnings

*Come let us go up to the mountain of the LORD,*
*to the house of the God of Jacob.*
Micah 4:2

*...Even them I will bring to My holy mountain, and make*
*them joyful in My house of prayer. Their burnt offerings*
*and their sacrifices will be accepted on My altar; for My*
*house shall be called a house of prayer for all nations.*
Isaiah 56:7

2004 was a difficult year; it was the year I left Iris Ministries. Difficulties arose among the Mozambicans so that some of them could no longer work with Iris. Much repentance was needed. For me, a decision had to be made. I remembered that in Israel my Messianic brothers would be upset when internationals would go back home when times were tough. I couldn't leave the Mozambican people that God had called me to partner with. I needed to continue with them, to struggle with them, and to pray it through with them.

After six years of laboring together for the Kingdom, parting with Iris Ministries, and particularly with Rolland and Heidi, was incredibly hard. But there was only love and care between us personally, and they gave me a beautiful farewell bouquet. I can only praise God for all their support and teaching. I praise God too for the way the Lord continues to use them in so many countries now around the world. So many children's lives are saved, both physically and spiritually, through their tireless efforts.

Now I had to learn again to trust the Lord every day. During this year, God gave me a wonderful vision in a dream that brought me much comfort and peace. I was driving my truck, full of my Mozambican brothers and sisters on a dirt road. In front of us was a beautiful forest.

There was no rough ground or thistles, just beautiful slender trees. I suddenly reached a steep decline and had to slam on the brakes coming to a screeching halt and found myself in a very dangerous situation. God said, "Look up." Among the tops of those beautiful trees, I saw a man in a brown robe looking at me. By his side was a lion that he was leading by a golden cord. It

*Pulled manually, a barge transports the MOP church team across a river. I am the driver of the truck secured with only the breaks.*

was so peaceful. At first I thought it was an angel, and I heard the Lord say, "Look again." Then it became clear to me that this was my Lord Jesus in His brown earthly tunic, in full control of a lion. He is the Peace in the storm.

Prior to all these events, the Lord had spoken to me about doing a "new thing." I did not know at the time what this meant, but now this "new thing" was upon me. I was stepping out in missions without the support of a bigger group and working much more closely with local people. Four words came clearly to me: teach, equip, empower, release. I felt the Lord telling me to let the Mozambicans lead. I was not to lead the way but to walk *beside* them, praying and fasting with them.

Now that I was the only foreigner, not everything was easy. However, my Mozambican church family were so good to me and so thoughtful in many ways. On mission trips into the bush when living conditions were basic and there were many difficulties to overcome, they always made sure that I had a Mozambican sister with me. I had much to learn on how to do things.

My faithful home church again supported me, and their support for the orphans we were caring for grew and grew. The Mozambican church set up a new organization, ACPO (the Christian Association for the Support of Orphans), which also included care for widows, and blessed individuals from my home church began sponsoring children. One mother wrote to me about her two-year-old child, "If I don't pray for them, she says, 'Pray children in Bique.'"

The Lord did not forget my own personal need of emotional and spiritual support. Towards the end of the year, I attended a singles retreat in South Africa run by my dear friends Yanit and Reuven. I had to travel by bus from Maputo, and I was late arriving. Everyone was already sitting at dinner at beautifully set tables. It was very festive, being near Christmas. I came in and sat at the table, and I just wept from the pain and struggle of the last year. Through that weekend, Yanit and Reuven listened to me, coming alongside me with prayer and counsel. They gave me a copy of an article called "The Joseph Anointing." It helped me to understand how Joseph had had to go through many very difficult things in order for God's greater purpose to be done. Sometimes, in the process, God allows painful separations in relationships. This was so healing for me.

During this time, the Lord blessed me with another vision. I have found it is often at times of the greatest difficulty that Jesus comes so close to me. I saw our Father God's eyes in a dream one night. I was walking, and then I stopped. I saw only His eyes—awesomely loving, gleaming, nearly piercing, yet so gentle, so compassionate. I then saw His upper body, and He was clapping for me, as a father might do when praising or encouraging his child at play. His eyes were full of joy for me. He then spoke, "Keep going, daughter. Keep going."

In the weeks and months after the parting from Iris ministries, we would gather together as church on Sunday mornings. There was much prayer and repentance. At first Pastor Rego felt he could not lead a new church. Later on, a group of us went further into the countryside

*Emblem of Mountain of Praise church based on Micah 4:1-2. "Come, let us go up to the mountain of the Lord...."*

where we have farms that help support the orphan work. We spent three days in fasting and prayer, and on our return, we continued for another ten days.

The Lord worked very deeply in my own heart. He gave me Micah 4:1-2 alongside Isaiah 56:7, which became the key verses for the founding of the Mountain of Praise Church, which is now a recognized denomination in Mozambique.

*Pastor Rego leads the MOP church through rice fields to a baptism.*

Now it shall come to pass in the latter days that the mountain of the Lord's house shall be established on the top of the mountains, and shall be exalted above the hills; and peoples shall flow to it. Many nations shall come and say, "Come, and let us go up to the mountain of the Lord, to the house of the God of Jacob; He will teach us His ways, and we shall walk in His paths." For out of Zion the law shall go forth, and the word of the Lord from Jerusalem. (Micah 4:1-2)

Even them I will bring to My holy mountain, and make them joyful in My house of prayer. Their burnt offerings and their sacrifices will be accepted on My altar; for My house shall be called a house of prayer for all nations. (Isaiah 56:7)

This is a wonderful end-time prophecy of what the Lord will do with the nations. Any people group that has suffered so long as Mozambique has may have the tendency to look inward and to pray only for their concerns. I felt God was saying it was time to look upward and outward. He wanted Mozambicans to pray His heart of love and redemption not only for their country, but also for Israel and other nations, and to send out Mozambican ambassadors and evangelists.

At the end of our retreat, the men came together in praise, raising their hands together in a circle, forming a "mountain" with their raised hands. It was a time of great encouragement as we began to move on in this new phase.

*2005: The MOP church is baptizing new believers in a small river flowing through a rice field.*

## From Yanit Ross, Christian author, counselor, teacher, and long-time friend

We first met Tanneken in Israel when she joined a singles ministry we had set up in Jerusalem. When we moved up to Haifa to help David and Karen [Davis] in Haifa, we were surprised to find Tanneken there also. We worked together in the women's shelter; I would do some teaching and ministry there, and she was always a part of that, sitting in on that. I remember her pouring her life out for those people and wanting to learn from me. She wanted to learn anything she could and try to put it into practice.

Our friendship developed as we worked together. In Israel, we were so short of laborers, and we all worked so hard in building the Lord's kingdom, we often didn't work to build friendships, but they often develop as you're thrown in the same ministry. That's what it was like with Tanneken. As she prepared to go to Africa, we spent more time together as I had lived in Africa for seven years, and I was able to give her the "heads-up" on what it might be like for her there. My husband Reuven and I hosted her farewell party.

Later on we also returned to work in [South] Africa and helped staff a singles conference one Christmas. We hadn't seen Tanneken for some years. Tanneken arrived at that full of malaria, high with fever.

She was the last missionary to arrive just as we were sitting down to dinner. I jumped up from my place and ran over and hugged her, and man, she was so hot.

We got her a plate of food and were about to hold hands to pray over the food. Tanneken looked down and started crying, telling us her children at home did not have enough to eat, and how someone had gone to the river to look for edible roots just to feed their children and had been attacked by crocodiles. We all just looked at our food and cried with her, and thought, how are we going to eat our food? Tanneken just started eating. She cried her tears, she said her story, but she then said she was thankful for this food: "Thank you, Jesus, and let's eat."

Part of my role for that week was to be a counselor for the missionaries that had come, and I got to give extra time to Tanneken. We were just there for her, pastoring and helping her pray it through. When you go through a major change like Tanneken had, it can take a while just working through, praying through. I think we did more of that when we saw her the next year. Looking back, we've been there at very significant times for Tanneken.

## More from Steve Chupp

As her pastor, I have been honored to walk alongside Tanneken during her struggles and triumphs. During a time of serious misunderstanding and loss of relationship in Mozambique, we often prayed together and sought God's wisdom in how to move forward. In each situation, Tanneken was willing to do whatever God asked. She grieved the losses and sought Jesus to heal the pain, refusing to harbor bitterness or unforgiveness. And God responded by providing all she needed to joyfully move on.

# Building the House of the Lord

*Stein auf Stein, Stein auf Stein,*
*das Haus das wird bald vertig sein.*
*Stone upon stone, stone upon stone*
*and the house will soon be finished.*
A German rhyme from my childhood

*Unless the* Lord *builds the house, they labor in vain*
*who build it; unless the* Lord *guards the city,*
*the watchman stays awake in vain.*
Psalm 127:1

SEPTEMBER 2007—DONDO, MOZAMBIQUE

It is early Friday morning at this lovely property with a heart-shaped little garden in the center of the property, with the words, "Garden of Eden" written with little pebbles. Our 16 boys in their new dormitory and six girls (eight on weekends) in my home are rising at 5 am, and now once more beginning the day with songs of praise. The early school group leaves at 6 am; others are watering the flower gardens, chopping wood for the fire, cleaning the chicken coop, cleaning their dormitory, washing their clothes, taking baths and finally having their breakfast of corn-mush or sweet potatoes grown in our garden. It is a delight to see precious lives grow into children and adolescents, learning to live as a family, care for one another, help one another, respect one another, go to school willingly, and most of all become children of God. They know that even though they are orphans, they have a heavenly Father who loves them and truly, "sets the solitary in families" (Psalm 68:6a).

Right now I hear Paulo, our ten year old orphan—who was an abandoned child found by a person working for the government in a remote village—drawing water from the well, singing. I see Lino—who I found dirty and dressed in rags five years ago on the streets of Beira—who in these past years was dealing with a severe anger problem but now is really calming down, today energetically digging up the sweet potatoes and planting new ones.

I see Fatima, our 11 year old girl, living with illness, leading the girls in early morning prayers, sweeping the outdoors, going to school, and in general in better health than ever before.

I see Alberto, our 16 year old orphan youth—who came to us years ago tired of begging food on the streets, asking if he and his brothers and sister could live with Papa Rego—now a transformed teenager, who is helping Jose in the new dormitory as assistant staff leader for the younger orphan boys, leading the evening prayers with all the orphan boys that live here at the center and singing actively in the Unity of Churches youth choir.

I wrote these words above in a newsletter home. In the years since stepping out on my own in missions, the Lord had built a home. A home is so much more than the physical building, although that is very important too. A home is a place to feel safe, to settle, for children to flourish and grow, where they can become what God intended them to be. My vision was for a more permanent home that could be shared with widows and

These precious orphan girls live at my house located in Dondo.

Orphan girls, delighted by the beauty of the morning glories, look through the security bars on my veranda. After decades of war and suffering, the first president of Mozambique, Semora Machel, proclaimed that "Children are flowers that never wilt."

*Widow Fanita (sitting in front of a store) walked with the youngest orphans into Dondo to buy them their first pair of shoes.*

*2005: The orphans piled into my truck are waving happily because they just received new shoes.*

orphans. With the support of my home church Zion Chapel, and many other brothers and sisters, we were able to buy a beautiful piece of land with 23 mango trees and 14 coconut palms. Over a couple of years, the house began to be built. Every week, we met on the property to pray God's protection and purposes.

Teams from my own church and others began to come and help build. It was a great blessing to have my brother Hans and his wife Vera, together with Art and Joyce Friesen, come from Port Rowan Community Church in Canada. With great skill, they fitted all the window security bars for my house, which was not just my residence but included four bedrooms that housed girl orphans and the mamas who cooked for them and oversaw their care. Hans also installed swings and a roundabout in our compound; no other roundabout existed in the whole of Dondo! This simple playground equipment has been such a blessing to the children over the years.

Over the years the work included other buildings on the compound. Hans and Vera returned a couple of years later with a team of 17, and they built a dormitory for 20 boys with bunk beds and a veranda, as well as a separate bath house (but no outdoor plumbing). My brother Mel and his wife Janet also helped in various generous ways, so I really felt the support of my brothers and their wives. Many faithful Christians from my home church and many other churches helped build a security wall around the entire compound and an outdoor cement block kitchen (the orphans' kitchen) that replaced a rickety stick-and-mud shelter under a grass roof. It was all done in obedience to God's word as written in James 1:27, "Pure and undefiled religion before God and the Father is this: to visit orphans and widows in their trouble and to keep oneself unspotted from the world."

The Lord provided in another way too with the arrival of Claudia, a teacher for deaf children from Germany. Claudia helped us to establish a small elementary school for our two deaf orphans, and other children from the Dondo community. Marjan and Daniel were both able to hear and speak until they were around five years old. They were then struck with an illness which caused their deafness. Both came to us not speaking or hearing, but God restored their speech. However, they were not able to go to school, as the local public schools had no program for deaf children. As a result of Claudia's diligent and successful efforts, Daniel and Marjan are today successfully studying at a school for deaf children in Beira, which I believe to be the only school for the deaf in the nation.

Every evening, all our orphans meet together with the older boys to hear a Bible story and to pray together. One evening, as all the children gathered for their evening prayers, Pastor and Mama Rego, sitting outside their home, heard Marjan singing in Portuguese, "Jesus pasando por aqui" (Jesus is passing by this way). Marjan then asked for the Scripture booklet, "The Way to God," turned to the page where Jesus is on the cross and started preaching: "We must be kind to one another; we must not hit one another; it is good to have food, and even if our food is not always so tasty, God will always care for us; Jesus is close by us, praying for us."

The next Sunday, after praying for Marjan, pastor Rego said that God can speak through all of us, also through the children, and that we should never belittle them. Then he invited Marjan to speak at church. Marjan, Scripture booklet in hand, with Antonio as his interpreter, sang two songs and spoke a similar message. People were amazed! It was very special to see this deaf child inspired by the Holy Spirit to speak so clearly these childlike but true words.

Of course we faced great sadness at times, witnessing at first hand the suffering that diseases such as AIDS and malaria have caused so many people. Members of our church regularly visit people in their

*After hearing the Gospel, a witch doctor converted and brought all his instruments to be burned, including a guitar. What a day of delivery and rejoicing!*

homes who are sick, or who have lost loved ones, and pray with them. We prayed frequently for one young woman who was dying of AIDS. A few weeks before her death, we were able to bring her to a prayer meeting, where she confessed that she had gone to the witch doctor and false prophets for healing and really wanted to break with that.

Consulting witch doctors, ancestor worship, and engaging in witchcraft hold many people in bondage and under curses in Mozambique. Cords are often put round infants' necks and wrists. The witch doctors are paid for this in the belief they will offer protection from disease and evil spirits. When people come to convert we often see these cords on their children. We explain these won't protect their children and point to Jesus, who loves us, who alone can offer us protection. Then we ask to cut the cords. When they are cut and we pray, it is wonderful to see peace come over them.

Just a few days before her death, this young woman read the Bible together with her father, who was not a Christian. The day before her death, I visited her with a few other ladies from the church. She was not able to respond. As we sang, "Father, here we are waiting for you," she started breathing more heavily and lifted her hand up to me. I lay next to her on her reed mat, laid my head on hers and just whispered in her ears that Jesus loves her. Twelve hours later she left this earth, and was home with the Lord, free of all suffering and pain.

Another time I was at a graduation, a festive occasion for our Bible school students, when I received a phone call. "Mama, please come quickly with your truck. The school teacher that lives close to the Regos' home says she wants to go to the hospital."

I didn't really want to leave the celebrations, but I knew I had to do what God was calling me to do, or I would have no peace. This teacher had suffered for weeks from a prolonged illness. For days, she could not eat and could hardly talk. Her body was wracked with AIDS. We laid her into the back of my Isuzu truck and brought her to that dinky third-world type hospital in Dondo. They had already sent her home, telling her that they could do no more for her, but since she asked, we brought her. As we were taking her out of the truck, she said with her last strength, "Maaa-maaa-maaaa."

I said, "What do you need?" She could not answer.

I laid down beside her, placed my hand on her head, and said to her, "Jesus loves you. Just say to Him that you are sorry."

With her last breath, she said in Portuguese, "I am sorry."

I continued to comfort her and simply said, "Your life is in Jesus' hands; He loves you very much." We carried her into the hospital and left her with two of the brothers. I returned to the graduation. Two hours, later I heard that she had died. She asked for forgiveness and now entered her eternal home. I was at peace and felt joy in my heart.

The Lord showed me again how important it is to follow His call, His leading and to stop for the one that needs help. I do not know how to express this, but it seemed as if she could not die until someone came to give her an opportunity to say "I am sorry, Jesus." Yes, I had to leave a fun graduation, but that is nothing compared to the joy that a sinner is home with Jesus, forever!

Losing one of our own children was a cross that was very hard to bear, but thankfully, it happens very rarely. Fatima, who I described above in my newsletter lived with us for three years. She arrived with her sister and cousin, and when I first met her, she was huddled in a corner, crying, "I want to go home to my sister." I sat down next to her, drew her close to myself and tried to comfort her, telling her that God had now given her a new family with Mama and Papa Rego and the Mountain of Praise Church orphan care center. I promised to give her a capulana (a simple cloth used to wrap around the waist like a skirt) and a scarf to cover the sores on her head. With that promise, she finally calmed down, and our friendship began.

When my new home was built, Fatima, her sister, and cousin moved in. They were so excited! For the first time in their lives, they slept in a bed. I heard Fatima's sister calling her Tanni. They explained that her real name was Fatima, but she was nicknamed Tanni. This was extra special to me since my childhood nickname was also Tanni.

Fatima came to us unwell. Twice a day, she had to take a tablet to combat the illness that she in her innocence suffered from. She struggled to take this bitter tasting pill. I tried various ways to help her take it more easily. We counted in different languages, including German, "Eins, zwei, drei." On "drei," she took that medication. One day, she came to me a pill in one hand, a cup of water in the other, a

*Orphan girls enjoying breakfast—porridge made with corn meal and a little sugar. Left front is Fatima Tanni who suffered a prolonged illness and is home with the Lord.*

*Fatima Tanni at about eight years old*

smile on her face. She said, "Look Mama, eins, zwei, drei." She took that pill without struggle and down the hatch it went.

Inwardly, I sometimes cried for Fatima, hearing her cry of pain, as the aunties (our widows that helped care for her) and the other children cleaned her sores and covered them with bandages. Many a time she complained of stomach aches and diarrhea. We fed her rice instead of corn mush and vegetables or fish instead of beans. I would take her in my arms and pray with her and she would then calm down.

Fatima had the gift of prayer. I rarely heard a child pray the way she talked with "Baba," her Father in Heaven. She loved Bible stories. When I came into their bedroom to say goodnight, I sometimes saw her and her sister Zinia reading Bible stories out of our children's Bible story book. Sometimes in the early mornings, she came to me and told me her dreams. Even though some of her dreams were scary, they frequently ended in a good way. A few times, she had dreams of angels, and I reminded her to try and remember those. We prayed that she would not remember the bad part of the dream but only the good part.

One time she came running home from school very scared and upset. It was already dark and she had been alone in a thunderstorm and had to ask a lady along the way if she could find shelter under her roof. Then she heard God's voice saying, "Don't be afraid, for I am with you." As she told me this, her little fast beating heart calmed down, and I assured her that God had already spoken to her, that she was already in His hands, and that He protected her day and night.

The last months of Fatima's twelfth year on earth were her best. She had no sores, so much so, that she asked me if I would buy her for her birthday the pretty long black artificial hair, which one of her friends could then braid into her lovely tight little black curls. Fatima had a sponsor, whom she knew as Auntie Anna from my home church, Zion Chapel, and she looked so pretty in the dresses that Anna sent her.

One holiday, she went to visit her grandma and her aunt. She returned happily, but told me that her throat was hurting. That evening, she went together with all the other children to our church where she danced with Shanee, a precious girl from Israel who had visited us with her parents Gidon and Renee and her brother Avichai. Fatima had such a gift of dance and learned the Israeli dance steps quickly.

Little did we know that two days after this, her life would end, and that she would dance in Heaven, free from suffering from this horrible plague. Fatima taught me so much about overcoming suffering and trusting God the way she did in her years of suffering. She was so much part of our large children's family, going to school, sweeping the yard, washing her clothes, helping the aunties clean the dishes, scrubbing the pots and pans, playing jump rope, singing and dancing in church. God's ways are much higher than our ways, and His timing is always right, even when we do not understand. Just as Fatima trusted God in the time of the storm, she taught me to continue to trust in Him.

Our fledgling church, Mountain of Praise, grew and grew. Many individuals and congregations joined us and new churches were planted. By the end of the first year, there were over 400 Mountain of Praise (Igreja Monte de Louvor) churches. Slowly, a national church leadership was being formed. Besides Pastor Rego, the Lord gave us many wise and godly leaders. Pastor Tomo cannot read, but memorizes Scripture and preaches from those verses or passages. Now he is our National Counselor. He and his wife work as a team to offer counsel and prayer, particularly to married couples. He has helped us as well with our teenage orphans.

Pastor Rego and Pastor Tomo traveled all over the Sofala province preaching and encouraging the churches. Their main message was to love the Lord and to forgive one another. Some churches were made out of mud; some met under mango trees. I often traveled to remote areas with them and other church members to visit and encourage these congregations. We were always met with joy, witnessing people with such a heart of praise, coming up the mountain as it were, finding Christ.

*Fatima Tanni's last angel drawing before she went home to be with Jesus*

We felt the Lord's hand of protection on those journeys. The Malapansi Church in Marromeu is a three-hour drive, much of it along a narrow and bumpy dirt road that is often made impassable in the tropical storms that blow up so quickly there. The skies were dark as we set out on the only day we could make this trip, and we prayed for the Lord to contain the rain. Not a single drop of rain fell! When we arrived, the believers were gathered, dancing, full of joy that we had really come. On our return, we saw heavy rain had fallen on the sugar cane fields, but had stopped exactly where the dirt road had started!

Claudia was with me on one mission trip to Malawi. It was some days' journey with stops at our partner churches along the way. I became very ill with a kidney infection, perhaps the closest I have come to dying. On the second day we arrived at Chemba, and I was so sick, unable to take food or even water. The pastors prayed for me and I was cared for by precious women. Claudia was very worried for me and asked if we should not turn back, but in prayer it was decided to keep on with the mission.

After the third day I started to be able to keep water down and we drove onto Bangula in Malawi. I was feeling a little better, but I could hardly walk. They rushed me to a doctor to receive emergency treatment. As I came out of the clinic I met Desi Jacob, with one of the orphans he was working with in Malawi. Desi prayed for me and found out where we were staying, visiting me again and caring for me so faithfully. Desi and his wife Martha have become dear friends, and through them other churches and friends have been touched to help us over the years.

The church grew across borders, and Pastor Gent of Bangula, Malawi, became our national co-ordinator for Malawi and was responsible for around 45 churches. From the beginning, Pastor Gent was a godly, dedicated church leader. When he heard that a new church was being founded in Mozambique, he traveled all the way to Dondo, not knowing where we were gathered for a time of fasting and prayer. With help from folks in Dondo, he found us gathered in Mudima, Manica, a very remote village where the Regos had started planting corn fields. Next to their mud huts, where we found shelter, there was a mud hut church, which the Assemblies of God allowed us to use while the new church was being founded.

Pastor Gent worked alongside Pastor Rego and was faithful in leading the foundation of this new church. He was also an anointed worship leader in congregational singing. One of his favorite songs was "Sienne, Molungu, Akale Molungo," meaning "If God is God then let Him be God." Sadly, this man of God, who preached the Word with great zeal, died in 2014. We truly miss him but know that he is among the cloud of witnesses, encouraging us on in the race as we follow Jesus.

Pastor Bizeque was also fundamental in our church's beginning, as he helped Pastor and Mama Rego first find the Lord.[1] He discipled Pastor Rego and gave his family shelter at one particularly dangerous time during the civil war. Sadly, he also died in 2014, but had served the Lord faithfully, becoming the Treasurer and the Coordinator of Prayer and Intercession for Mountain of Praise Church for many years.

Alongside their husbands are faithful women of God. Mama Pastora Rego is our national leader for women and also leads the orphan care program. She has been a friend and "mama" to me over many years. Every evening when I lived with the Regos in their small home, she cleaned the lamps and lit them so that I could work on my computer.

*I am preaching in the MOP church in Bangula, Malawi. This church building is made of sticks, mud and a grass roof tied together with vines.*

*I am preaching in Bangula, Malawi.*

*I am praying for the sick in a remote church made of sticks and grass.*

*2015 - At the request of the Dondo municipality, Pastor Rego preached the Word of God about the peace that only Jesus can give.*

We had to learn to know each other, as our cultural backgrounds were so different. Bit by bit, we came to a better understanding and today we are good friends and sisters in the Lord.

It took Mama Rego some years to step into the role of a pastor's wife and realize her value to both her husband and the church in that position. But today she is a vital part of the Mountain of Praise national leadership team and works confidently alongside our pastors and other faithful women: Mama Conselhera Tomo, Mama Evangelista Gabriel, Mama Secretaria White and Mama Tresorera Bizeque.

Pastor Rego is much respected in the local community and with local officials. In May 2005, our church was invited to receive Senhora Maria da Luz Guebuza, the wife of the President of Mozambique. Our sisters lifted their hands in worship, and Pastor Rego was able to pray God's blessing, protection, and wisdom for the president and his wife. One of our children gave their "First Lady" a carving of a Mozambican child kneeling in prayer. We heard later how touched Senhora Guebuza was that her welcome to Dondo was done in prayer. This is from a government that was Marxist. Two government officials spoke with Pastor Rego and came to Christ on that same day. Hallelujah!

The Lord brought me back to the calling He gave me, to teach, equip, empower and release the nationals, to not lead from in front but to encourage them and spur them on for the Kingdom. He gave me another vision to make this clear to me. I saw myself and Pastor Rego with a great crowd of people. Ahead of us was a great ravine with a river flowing through, which we had to cross. A bridge came into view that was not level, but sloped steeply upwards. I went ahead with Pastor Rego with a hammer in my hand, and we started climbing.

All the people followed, but it was frightening; the bridge had no rails to hold onto. One in the crowd called out, "Mama, stop! This is dangerous; we must go back!"

"No, Jesus called us to cross this river," I replied. "We must keep going." We did and crossed the river safely. In difficult times, this was a reminder to me that it was very important to encourage the leaders to press on, to help them see that present trials can be overcome.

It is a great blessing to see our local church reaching out to others in love and prayer. Each week, a group goes into the local hospital to pray with the sick and the dying. We offer prayer and a Scripture booklet if people wish, and people are so receptive. On one occasion, doctors and nurses knelt in the corridor asking us for prayer. On another occasion, as we were going from room to room, two doctors were giving medications. We introduced ourselves and asked if we might pray for the patients. Their answer was amazing: "Yes, please enter. Prayer is more important than medicine."

Within the orphan ministry, we are now seeing youth who started with us as little children now taking responsibility in leading the new children. It's a real blessing to see this happen and an encouragement to me that the Lord will carry on His work when I cannot continue. There was still much work to do in establishing and encouraging this new church. Once again I would know the support of my home church and other dear friends in carrying out this Kingdom task.

## Mama Pastora Cicilia Rego, Mountain of Praise Church

I thank God that He was able to touch Mama Tanneken to come to us here in Mozambique. And yes, Mama Tanneken has a deep calling from the Lord. She has a will and desire to serve the Lord here in Mozambique—to help the mission, together with the mission to orphans.

God knew Mama Tanneken before she was born. He knew everything about Mama Tanneken because she was chosen from the time she was in the womb of her mother. Without this calling she could not do anything. A person must have the will to serve others. In this way the work in a mission goes well. I always pray that God blesses Mama Tanneken where she works, where she walks and where she sleeps. May the Lord always be the Key for her. We are not only friends but we are family. Thank you!

## José, accountant for Mountain of Praise Church

I lived with my parents in Savane [very remote village], where they didn't have secondary schools. So I came to Dondo to live with my uncle and attend secondary school. My uncle was a nurse and worked away, so I mainly lived with my aunt. My father always encouraged me, since I was living with their family, to do everything as a son of the house. I went home on occasion, but when I came back, there was gossip from the aunt, who said I had stolen things from the aunt. She didn't accuse me directly, she always went by the neighbors. I never stole anything. The root of it was that she didn't want me to live in the house.

I told my father this, and my father went to Pastor Rego. Pastor Rego said that I could live with them in order to continue my studies. I did not know Mama Tanneken at the time, but my father said, "You must live as if it is your own home, as if you are a son there and help with everything that you would help with at home." That is how I started to get to know Mama Tanneken.

As I was living [with] her, I noticed that she was a mama to the children, to the youth, to the adults, to everybody. In the beginning, I didn't help her much, but she helped me a lot. She saw that I liked to help with the children. [Pastor Rego trusted José very early on, he was always being trusted with money and sent to the market.]

One time, Tanneken was very sick in the hospital with malaria. She needed to contact her brother, and she asked me to write a message on the computer. I have never used a computer before. I succeeded in writing this message, and I showed more interest. I continued on to take a computer course in the municipality, and Tanneken paid for this. Our mama loves to delegate and see the gifting in others. While I was still studying, she talked to Pastor Rego, and both of them agreed to train me to become the accountant for our ministry. I studied for one year and the ministry paid for the transport and the monthly fees. I continued with success. Now I am the accountant for the orphan ministry and the church.

## Lorenzo, student, age 17

I live with Mama Tanneken [in the boy's dormitory in Tanneken's compound]. When I was twelve, my parents died and my grandfather brought me to this ministry. I have one brother and one sister, and they live here with me. I am currently in the tenth grade at school and in the midst of exams right now. I love biology, chemistry and physics, and when I am older, I would like to be a medical doctor.

I first lived with Pastor Rego, and I remember that Mama Tanneken would visit us there and would do many things with us, play with us, sing with us. She helped me to learn to sew with a machine and to sing in worship. I have learned to play the soprano recorder and the guitar. Mama helped me to learn English, to pray, and to stay firm in faith in the Lord.

Recently I went to Kidslink, an Australian ministry, to learn how to lead children, how to lead play activities, not to be rough or cruel, instead how to guide them and guard them well. We learned many Bible verses and games. They also gave me a reward, a new Bible.

God bless you. Have good dreams with God, have dreams of the Lord.

# World Missionary Press

*So shall My word be that goes forth from My mouth; it
shall not return to Me void, but it shall accomplish what I
please, and it shall prosper in the thing for which I sent it.*
Isaiah 55:11

The Scripture distribution ministry of World Missionary Press
(WMP)[1] has been such an important part of my ministry in Israel and
Mozambique. They produce Scripture booklets in over 300 languages,
giving them away free of charge. They don't even charge for shipping!
The booklets are purely Scripture quotes under various headings, so
they do not espouse any particular denomination's doctrine. Each
booklet contains the message of salvation according to the Word of
God. Ever since I got saved through a radio broadcast, I had such a
deep longing in my heart that I, too, could proclaim the Lord's mercy
and message of salvation, so I was drawn to these materials.

I first became aware of them when I was in Israel. I noticed we
had no appropriate materials from a Jewish perspective that used the
prophets of the Old Testament to point people to Jesus, the Messiah.
At that time, WMP gave me thousands of copies of a booklet called
"Wings over Zion." It used Old Testament quotes, pointing to Jesus as
the Messiah. I brought them to Israel, bit by bit in my suitcase, and
they were helpful for many people, becoming part of their journey
towards a fuller understanding of our Lord Jesus. In the late afternoons
and early evenings, we would go with the brothers and sisters from
our ministry to the streets to distribute these valuable booklets. Most
of the time, they were well received.

While still with Iris Ministries in Mozambique, I contacted WMP
again, and we received a large shipment of booklets. We have used
their booklet, "The Way to God" many, many times. Because of its clear
message of salvation by faith in Jesus Christ, along with illustrations,

this booklet has now been translated into three more of the principal African languages. We are proud of the nationals who gladly translated them without asking for payment. They are overjoyed that these booklets are now in their dialect.

Since over one million booklets were distributed by 2008, Mountain of Praise Church asked for a second shipment; they sent us a full shipping container—4,213 boxes, each containing around 500 booklets! They came in many languages: Portuguese, Sena, Makua, Shona, ChiChewa, and Tsonga, just a few of the 26 or more dialects of Mozambique. The huge, heavy metal container was purchased by WMP and given to MOP Church who was now going to be the WMP official distributor in Mozambique.

We had to wait a long time at Beira port, but finally, the container was loaded onto a rickety truck to be transported 20 miles or so to Dondo. Of course, the truck broke down and caused more delay. When it finally arrived, we couldn't afford a crane to move the container from the truck to its resting place on the compound where I live. Each box had to be unloaded by hand. Then the empty container was dragged off the truck with a chain and rolled into place on metal tubes pulled by the local municipality's tractor.

All our orphans, church folks, and neighbors helped unload and then repack the container. It took us two full days. Finally, all was ready, awaiting distribution bit by bit through our missions and other local churches.

Pastor Rego and I have worked as national coordinators for WMP and taken the booklets not only all over Mozambique but also into Zimbabwe and Malawi. In the Mozambican churches there has been better cooperation in this effort. The last shipment has brought many different denominations together, and that has been a great blessing. WMP has also sent us a coloring book for children called "God is Love" and "He is Risen," written in Portuguese; this has been of tremendous value to us in our children's work. Even prisoners have requested to receive the large coloring books. They have rarely or never seen an illustrated Children's Bible. The illustrations helped them to learn and remember the stories

One day, I was giving out some booklets with some of the youth of our church at a local gas station. There were about eight boys there. As they stood in a circle reading the tracts, I simply asked them: "Would you like to receive Jesus today? He loves you; He's here by His Holy Spirit. We can ask Him to come and live in our hearts. We need to

*Orphans are helping to load a container with World Missionary Press scripture booklets.*

confess that we are sorry for what we have done, but then He forgives us because He died on the cross for our sins. Let's follow Jesus." All of them accepted the Lord! We prayed that as those booklets went home with them, they would have more opportunity to think and pray about their decision.

Our church has developed a ministry of home visiting, often to older people or people who are suffering with AIDS. One such lady I have been privileged to visit is Mama Imaculada. She is now very old, but even when suffering painful arthritis, she used to walk for three hours with her rickety cane to come to MOP church. Now it is too much for her, and so we visit her. Some of her own children died, and she has raised six grandchildren, some of whom are married, others still completing school. I gave some Scripture booklets to Mama Imaculada's younger grandson, one who really looks out for his grandmother, saying that he could give some away to his friends in the neighborhood. He was keen to do this; he gave them all out and came back to me for more!

These precious Scripture booklets have been such a wonderful part of the Lord's work here in Mozambique, where Bibles can be in very short supply. I once visited some friends in Mafambisse, a town where there is a very large sugar cane factory. As I drove along, I felt

God speaking to me about going to the market to preach the Gospel, using our WMP booklets. The next week, I returned with two of our church's evangelists and some youth, and we did exactly what God told me to do. People came in crowds, all wanting a Scripture booklet. Soon a young man appeared, and before we knew it he invited us to his home. Now a church is planted in that young man's home! Brother Cordar, our youth leader, and brother Antonio Tomo, our district evangelist, go weekly to encourage the new believers.

I am so grateful to WMP, who not only send us the booklets but also cover our ministry with prayer, going the extra mile in their concern for our ministry. Before one Bible School with our church pastors, I mentioned to Marie at WMP the need for more discipleship material and more illustrated material to support teaching to those that struggle to read. Marie remembered some suitable materials by a partner organization, Every Home for Christ (EHC), and contacted them. By a divine appointment, a representative was currently in Mozambique visiting with pastor Anakleto, the EHC representative in Mozambique. I knew pastor Anakleto well, and so he gave us a generous 300 sets of these illustrated Bible study materials, all written in Portuguese.

We used them in the Bible School and then gave them to the pastors, particularly those in remote areas, where very few have Bibles. What an encouragement from the Lord! We use these materials to enhance our teaching of the Bible through storytelling, enabling the Gospel to be understood by many more people than perhaps simply using the written text.

The Lord says in Isaiah 55:11 that His Word will not return to Him void or empty but will accomplish what God purposed for it to do. Whenever somebody reads the Word, perhaps they are not yet saved and just put it away in a drawer. Yet I believe it will eventually be effective. So, regardless of how it is initially received, I am encouraged as we continue to give out these Scripture booklets. My experience in Mozambique has been that no one rejects the Scriptures. In fact, they all stretch out their hands and push themselves forward so that they will receive their copy.

Just before leaving on one of my trips back to America, I couldn't sleep; it was two in the morning. I asked the Lord to speak to me. He gave me these words from Deuteronomy 8:3: "Man shall not live by bread alone; but man lives by every word that proceeds from the mouth of the Lord." I asked the Lord, "Lord, what shall I do with this instruction of your Word to me?" I felt the Lord telling me to go to every soup kitchen, residential shelter, and the Salvation Army in my town and anywhere I traveled in America. I was to ask if they would be willing to include Scripture booklets in their food distribution programs.

So on my visits to America over the Christmas period, we have started this. My church has worked alongside the Salvation Army to fill food parcels and include two Scripture booklets, one being a Bible study. I pray that they believe in the Lord and get saved.

I travel quite often when back in America and at times use the train. On one journey from Chicago to Denver—through the awesome, snow-covered Rocky Mountains along the Colorado River—God opened the door to minister to an ex-drug addict. George, a 23-year old young man, sat in the seat in front of me. Conversation began and he told me that he was on the way to visit his mother who was suffering from cancer. An evangelist always looks for a small opening to share the love of God with someone, so I offered him the WMP Scripture booklet, "Help from Above." I gave him one to read and one for his mother. Only the Holy Spirit could have orchestrated all that happened from that moment on.

George shared with me that he had just served three months in prison for dealing drugs. He had tattoos on his arm, showing that he was a marijuana user, but he said, "I hate these." I then shared with him how Jesus died on the cross for all our sins. I asked him what the rosary that he was wearing meant to him. He said that it protects him. That was the door to share who our true Protector, Deliverer, and Savior is. He took the rosary off and kept asking me questions; he was so hungry to find a new life.

After a prayer of confession to the Lord that he did by himself, he said, "I feel so warm inside." That was another door to speak of God's forgiveness and great love for him as the Lord heard his prayers, forgave him, and now lives in his heart by the Holy

*I am wearing a Mozambican-style dress and enjoying sugar cane with a friend*

Spirit. He opened the "Help from Above" booklet. Pointing to the page where the reader is led to receive the Lord, he said, "Look, I just did this!" Our conversation ended with a prayer of confession, and this young man wanting to follow Jesus.

## Helen Williams, World Missionary Press

We were already supplying booklets for distributors in Mozambique and as our relationship with Tanneken grew, so did the frequency of shipments and quantity of booklets in each shipment. In 2008, Tanneken and Pastor Rego became our volunteer national coordinators for Mozambique, receiving and distributing boxes on behalf of WMP throughout the country. Tanneken is willing and eager to network with other ministries such as Every Home for Christ to help spread the Gospel throughout Mozambique and surrounding countries. She championed and helped facilitate the translation of the WMP coloring book, *God Loves You* from English into Portuguese.

Through our partnership, millions of portions of God's Word have been put in the hands of people throughout the country. Knowing that God's Word is alive and powerful, we expect many of these lives to be changed for eternity. The Scripture booklets have been a key component in the establishment and discipleship of believers throughout the country and the growth of the Mountain of Praise churches in the region. Tanneken has often spoken of the great influence and effectiveness of the coloring books in reaching the children.

Harold Mack, president of our organization, and his wife Marie are part of a prayer support group for Tanneken. They meet monthly to pray specifically for her and the ministry as well as supporting her in other ways. Since her sending church is in this area [Indiana], Tanneken visits World Missionary Press whenever she is in the USA. We are always impressed with her energy, enthusiasm, and charismatic personality. Her passion for "the least of these," the children and widows, has been a hallmark of her life.

# Firm Foundations

*...He will teach us His ways,
and we shall walk in His paths...*
Micah 4:2b

Mountain of Praise Church was growing, which was so encouraging, but I felt we needed help. Most of the pastors and leaders had had no biblical training. Pastor Rego had received his training through Iris Ministries, but now we were on our own. These leaders needed discipling, but we had no resources. All we had in Dondo was a little mud church. I prayed that the Lord would send His messengers with healing and restoring words for a church and a nation that was just getting on its feet after decades of war and suffering.

I talked with Pastor Rego about Reuven and Yanit Ross, my dear friends in Israel who had supported me so much over the years and who had a ministry of discipleship.[1] We agreed to plan an annual conference and to ask Reuven and Yanit if they would be willing to teach and mentor us using their own materials based on the Sermon on the Mount in Matthew 5, 6, and 7. They agreed to come, and our first annual church conference was held in June 2006. It was planned to fit around the planting and harvest season. July is winter in Mozambique, a time when our pastor-farmers would be able to leave their fields.

Over 230 pastors from Mozambique came as well as a couple from as far as Malawi and Zimbabwe. Reuven and Yanit came for 11 days and brought Adriana, a gifted Bible teacher, who was part of their ministry. The three-day conference was tremendously blessed. The pastors had an opportunity to give short reports about developments in their cities and congregations, so everyone was informed and encouraged. Reuven and Yanit preached the Word through translators with wisdom, not falling back on foreign clichés that local people would not understand. At the end of each teaching session, Pastor Rego gave a summary presentation in Masena, the local language, emphasizing the key points in a way that was best understood for the pastors.

God moved marvellously. At one session, a woman confessed to using witchcraft and asked for prayer to break this practice. We also dealt with other major issues. Reuven, Yanit, and I stood together at the altar, publicly asking for forgiveness for the wrongs that white people have committed over the centuries to our black brothers and sisters. Some pastors wept at the altar while others cried out for mercy; others forgave and cried out for more love.

The conference's impact was felt beyond our congregations. The local mayor of Dondo came to the concluding service, where Reuven spoke on the baptism of the Holy Spirit. The shofar he had brought from Israel was blown, and we felt a holy moving of God. Some people cried; some spoke in a new heavenly prayer language; some quietly prayed for more of Jesus while others proclaimed God's power and victory. This must have had an effect on the mayor, because later Pastor Rego was asked to pray at Dondo's 20th anniversary celebration and to dedicate a new conference building. Pastors from various congregations walked around the whole building, marking the doors and windows with a cross while praying.

This yearly conference has become an established part of our church's program and a real highlight in the year for all our pastors. Of course, there are costs involved. Because most of our pastors and leaders can't afford to pay for their transport to and from the conference, we provide the cost of transport and feed all them for a week. Again we felt the generosity of our church partners. Highland Baptist Church of Waco, Texas, supports Reuven and Yanit Ross. They have helped for many years to finance this vital aspect of our ministry and discipleship.

Marriage and fidelity has been a regular focus at each conference. Most marriages here are common law marriages consisting of a simple agreement between families and a payment from the husband to the wife's family. With so many difficulties around unfaithfulness and prostitution in our communities, we felt it was important that these marriages have the blessing of God and that there was a Christian testimony behind it. I had done various weddings with Rolland and Heidi as we married many couples while I was with their ministry. This helped us to continue doing these weddings, simple as they were.

So, at our annual conferences, we have a large marriage ceremony and invite couples to go through a service of commitment to each other in a Christian context. Scriptures are read relating to marriage; questions are asked of the bride and groom as in most marriage ceremonies, and promises are made to each other. Pastor Rego blesses their marriage and each couple takes communion together. Mama Rego lights two candles, which the couple hold to light a third candle, blowing out the other two, signifying that they are one.

One year, 36 couples participated. They are often too shy to hold hands or kiss in public, as it is not common to do that here. Pastor Rego and Pastor Tomo have to demonstrate with their wives how a man kisses a woman! It is a fun time and a very special time. There is nothing fancy: no fancy clothes, no cake, and sometimes a simple ring. Some years we have taken photos of them with their certificate as a sign of the seriousness of the commitment they have made.

At these conferences, we have also seen healings and deliverances. One lady asked for prayer after having been unable to have children for nine years, something which is very difficult to live with in all cultures, but can bring particular shame in Mozambique. Reuven prayed for her, and the following year, she attended with a baby in her arms. God heard her cry. She held up her precious son whom she named Reuven in thankfulness for the prayer he prayed over her.

*Yanit Ross is preaching at an MOP Church national conference in Dondo. I am translating into Portuguese.*

Bibles are in very short supply in many of our churches. Each year, Reuven and Yanit raised funds for Bibles and gave them out at the end of the conference. What joy the pastors expressed as they sang and danced upon receiving their own Bible, as well as copies of the teachings.

*Pastors are joyfully receiving their first Bible at an MOP Church conference.*

However, after a few years, we felt that for many of our pastors, three days was not enough. Also many struggled with literacy and needed a different way of teaching. I talked and prayed this over with Reuven and Yanit, and we felt that a longer teaching period was needed. Pastor Rego was keen for this also, so in 2011, we started our first Bible school. Following the conference, 29 men and 4 women stayed on to complete four weeks of teaching. I found some simpler teaching materials from the Satellite Bible College International in South Africa. Much of it was already translated into Portuguese and even Chichewa, which would service our churches from Malawi.

Yanit and Reuven stayed on a little longer to help, and Pastor Rego and his son Zito also taught. Our students worked so hard; worship and prayer were part of every day, with Mondays dedicated to prayer and fasting. Patrick is a brother from Zimbabwe who converted from Zionism, a religion that mixes Christian teaching with traditional beliefs including witchcraft. He spoke of how the Bible school had helped him:

> Bible study helps us to understand the Word of God. The Bible helps us to have good manners, living pleasing to God. The Bible teaches people to pray to God and to Jesus. It shows us the way to Jesus. We believe in God through the words that come from the Bible. The Bible corrects me when I go wrong. So the Bible is the best preacher in my life.

Reuven and Yanit's commitment to this teaching over many years helped give our church stronger foundations. My home church helped generously with finances, and with that support the church applied to the government to become a recognized denomination within Mozambique. This comes back to my calling to teach, equip, empower, and release. Mountain of Praise is a Mozambican church with a Mozambican leadership team, and, as such, is respected by the local people and the government. We can help through teaching and support, but for this to be a lasting witness for the Kingdom, it has to be owned and led by the people of Mozambique.

Reuven and Yanit's last year of ministry in Mozambique was in 2011. That year, they brought Charleeda Sprinkle, an experienced Bible teacher. In 2013, she became one of the teachers for the Bible school. We also sought out three trained Mozambican pastors to help teach alongside Pastor Rego and the late Pastor Gent from Malawi, wanting as much as possible to encourage local people to lead. There was political unrest in the country that year; the political group Renamo, who fought against the government in a long civil war, had taken up arms again, and our area of Sofala was their main stronghold. Only 26 students made it to the school. After 15 days of classes, 18 of them returned to their homes because their families were in danger, but we continued the school for the remaining few.

*I am teaching on evangelism in the MOP Church's grass roots Bible school. Two pastors are translating my Portuguese into Shona for the Zimbabweans and Masena for some of the elderly Mozambicans and Malawians.*

However, we struggled to help those with literacy difficulties. Some could not read and others labored to copy notes into their notebooks because as farmers, their hands are more used to a hoe than a pen or pencil. We also felt the material we were using was too advanced for them. Most of them did not know the basic Bible stories, so after the Bible school, we discussed what might work better. Tim Morningstar, the missions director at my home church in Indiana, suggested teaching the Bible through storytelling.

In 2014, things were quieter, and we had around 60 students. Around six left—again because of unrest in their villages—but others arrived and took their places. We were greatly encouraged by the increase in attendance, but every year, the potential for political unrest is always a prayer concern. Charleeda and I used the storytelling method. We selected 20 key stories from Genesis to Revelation to give them an overview of the whole Bible. Charleeda told the story, and I translated. Then she retold it by illustrating it with stick figure drawings on a white board. As she drew them, each student drew the same on a flashcard using few words.

Their picture cards became their "notes" for remembering all the parts of the story. In groups of two or three, the students then practiced telling the story to each other in their own languages. We had men and women groups using five different languages: Portuguese, Sena, Chichewa (for those from Malawi), and Shona and English (for those from Zimbabwe). It was so much fun and rewarding to watch every student retelling a Bible story they did not know before.

As our final exam, we asked each language group to dramatize a story from both the Old and New Testament. They passed with flying colors. The one part they didn't manage so well was learning the memory verse for each story. We also found that they had a hard time making life applications from the stories, but overall, this method proved to be very successful. The students learned many stories they had never heard before, and they gained confidence in knowing they could tell the story themselves.

We would love to have more attend the Bible school, but Pastor Rego can only invite as many as the funds raised allow as we have to provide food and transportation costs for every student. The school ended with a three-day pastors' conference, and 300 attended.

In 2015, the story telling continued with many more stories for second-year students. To save class time, picture cards were prepared for them to emphasize application and Scripture memory. All participants

*2015 Mission team to Malawi from right to left: Ed Wright, me, Mae Cicilia Rego, Pastor Rego, Pastor Tomo, Pastor Mende and Mae Joanice Gabriel.*

received continued teachings on Biblical Doctrine, Successful Christian Leadership, Praise-Worship-Prayer, and Evangelism as a Lifestyle. We also drove for two days to Malawi and held a pastors' conference for around 40 MOP churches there.

During these last few years, I noticed that age was slowing me a little, particularly in my knee, which had become arthritic. It was becoming an effort for me to keep going with my regular schedule of ten months in Mozambique, which included evangelistic trips, preparation for the pastors' conference and Bible school, and my main focus in overseeing the care of our orphans. But the Lord knew all this and took care of it in surprising ways. I was also to know His protection in the most terrifying circumstances.

## More from Yanit Ross

Being involved in the ministry of the Mountain of Praise churches and visiting Tanneken regularly in Mozambique has been a joy for Reuven and me. We have felt very blessed to partially sponsor and speak at the annual pastors' conferences in Dondo. We love their hunger for the Lord and His Word. Ministering alongside Tanneken is always a blessing for us; she is passionate about the Lord and His work, especially amongst the Africans!

Before one particular conference, the pastors had been praying and fasting for some days that God would confirm His Word with signs and wonders. One morning of the conference, Reuven taught on the pastor's role as the spiritual leader of his family as well as pastor of the church. I then taught on the woman's role—how she is to help her husband disciple women, counsel alongside him and pray with him for people, and intercede for him. At that time, most of the women were not taking an active role in ministry to others at all. Their focus was on raising the children, serving meals, and cleaning the house.

After I finished teaching, Pastor Rego arose to confirm our message. He encouraged all of us to walk in our ministries as couples. Then right above where we were sitting there was a very loud popping and cracking sound in the roof. The corrugated tin began to tear open. Initially, we thought someone was on the roof, ripping it open with tools, but there was no person up there. We quickly realized this was an act of God. The roof peeled back about the length of a meter [three feet], exposing the sun and sky. Light came in, shining directly on Reuven and me, and Pastor Rego cried out, "This is a miracle! This is God! He is confirming His Word!"

Soon afterward we broke for lunch, and most people were talking about the miracle we had just seen. When we returned to the church after lunch, the roof was mended, with only a slight crease in the metal where the tear had been. We wondered how the Mozambicans had mended the roof without us hearing any noise! Pastor Rego asked publicly if anyone had fixed the roof, but no one came forward. It was restored so perfectly that we realized that God had torn it open, and He had repaired it. Reuven and I had never seen anything like it! But, along with Tanneken, we know that God was confirming the truths that men and women are to minister together as couples. Since that time, more women have become involved in their husband's ministries.

During another conference, at the end of a day of teaching, a woman brought her 25-year-old son to the front of the church. He was demon-possessed and was destructive and violent at home. He was so demonized that he was out of control; he wanted help. There were six of us there to pray for him, including Tanneken and a few of the pastors. We led the young man in a salvation prayer, cast out the evil spirits, and then prayed with him to be baptized in the Holy Spirit. He was on his knees, and as He surrendered His life to Jesus, his whole countenance changed. There was some manifestation as the demons came out, but then he raised his hands and started worshipping the Lord. He looked clean and free and happy!

We invited him to come the following night when we were giving out Bibles. That evening I kept looking for him, praying he would come, and only saw him toward the end of the service. He was holding his new Bible, waving at me, tears running down his face, with a smile that stretched across his face. I marvelled at the change in that man in just 24 hours. What a difference Jesus makes in the lives of those who surrender to Him!

## From Charleeda Sprinkle, author, Bible teacher, missionary

I met Reuven and Yanit in Israel. In 2011, they invited me to join them on their annual ministry trip to Mozambique and assigned me topics to teach on for the pastors' conference. I also prepared flannelgraph stories for the children. This was my first trip to Africa. Walking through the village to the church was like walking through the pages of a *National Geographic* magazine! We did not know that would be Yanit and Reuven's last year there. The following year, I returned with them, but this time, we held a pastors' conference in Malawi and didn't go to Mozambique.

I learned about the Bible school that had started in 2011 and asked if it would be possible for me to help teach. Tanneken was thrilled at the prospect. In 2013, I taught some of the Satellite Bible courses they were using, but I found they were much too difficult for our students. Most did not have the basic knowledge of the stories of the Bible, so you could not teach theological topics, making references to Bible stories they didn't know. We needed to establish a course that would give them the basic knowledge of the Bible and present it in such a way that they could easily grasp it...without having to write notes.

In 2014, I wrote a curriculum outline of 20 basic Bible stories using stick figure drawings. We weren't sure how it would work. I'd never seen it done. I read through several similar type courses but none seemed simple enough. I started out by telling the story of the Bible from Genesis to Revelation in one class period. They had never heard this. They knew some stories but didn't know how they all fit together, and I was surprised that they had not heard many of the stories I told. To watch them break through their timidity (especially the women) and tell the stories to each other was truly an amazing sight to view.

There is nothing more wonderful for a teacher than having an eager, hunger group of students!

Though I'd lived overseas before, I'd never lived in conditions as difficult as I did in Mozambique. I didn't know how pampered this American was until 2013 when I stayed for seven weeks: cats underfoot because they catch the rats, massive swarms of ants collecting on the walls, taking malaria pills and sleeping under mosquito nets, taking bucket baths, sitting through a four-hour Sunday service with no air conditioning, living in community with orphans and widows, and squatting over simple holes in the ground were only a few of the things I had to get accustomed to.

Tanneken was so gracious and patient with my struggles. We're the same age, so I marvel at her ability to endure this lifestyle. It is NOT easy...though it seems not to bother her at all. It is so apparent to me that God had her future of living in Africa in mind when He gave her parents who lived the simple lifestyle of an Anabaptist community. She's definitely Mozambican, as African time doesn't faze her in the least! She cannot sit for long before her lap is full of dust-covered, runny-nosed children. They so love her! And she so loves them. She is a marvel to behold, a model of humble, loving sacrifice, and a joyful blessing to everyone around her.

# Unexpected Events

*God is our refuge and strength,*
*a very present help in trouble.*
Psalm 46:1

At the end of 2010, I had reached 65 years of age. My knee was slowing me down, but I was not ready to stop! Just before returning to America in early 2011, I accompanied our church leadership team on an outreach into Gorongosa, a remote area with many forests. We showed the *Jesus* film, and there was preaching into the night. The Lord worked in mighty ways and many were delivered of evil spirits and came to salvation in Jesus Christ.

Coming back I noticed an itching on my leg, and a dark blister formed by the ankle bone. I asked Pastor Rego what he thought, and he said, "I think you have been bitten by a snake." Sure enough, there were two clear marks at the bottom of the blister, as if the fangs of a snake had entered in. As I was not ill, I thought nothing of it. Ten days later, I left for America. The blister was still there, and on the plane I developed a fever.

I arrived home on a Friday and was shivering and sick, staying in my little flat on my own. On Sunday, I was expected in church, and Pastor Jim, our assistant pastor, came by to pick me up. I did not answer. He went on to church, but they became very worried for me. After church, Pastor Steve and his wife Ronda came to the flat with my neighbors Janet and Jerry, who had been away for the weekend. They found me in my night clothes, hardly able to walk or speak, collapsed on my couch.

They helped me to drink fluids, but at first, I could not keep them down. Janet cared for me and my doctor was called. Malaria tests proved negative. Then I remembered the bite and looked at the sore place on my left ankle. The blister had slowly disappeared. Now that the swelling had gone down, I saw two fang marks. I cannot know if it was the bite of a poisonous snake, but I am thankful for the Lord's protection! As He was with the apostle Paul He is with us as we step out and preach the Gospel.

Yet, perhaps also I needed to slow down. Because of the arthritis, the mission trips into the jungle were becoming difficult for me, and the ten months each year in Mozambique, with a rushed two months of visiting and speaking at my partner churches in America, was leaving me little time for rest. I could not imagine, however, spending less time in Mozambique.

On this same trip home in 2011, I was asked for a re-entry permit. I had been a legal permanent resident in America since 1963. I knew the rules and knew I needed to always come back within a year to maintain my residency. The officer kindly let me through without a re-entry permit. During this time in America, I traveled to Canada to visit some churches there. As I returned, I was stopped once more and made to stand aside in a waiting area. A search dog stood alongside an officer. I waited and waited and the time to board my plane was getting close.

Finally, an officer called me and was very gruff. "Mam, you cannot enter the States. Where is your re-entry permit?" I explained I did not know I needed one since the year had not yet expired. I had not heard that the law had changed. Now, apparently, permanent residents needed a re-entry permit after six months abroad to maintain their residency status. Just a few minutes before my flight's departure, the officer spoke with his manager and they gave me some forms that explained the changes in legislation. I was allowed through.

When finally home in Goshen, Indiana, I prayed with the mission team in church. To only be in Mozambique for six months of the year seemed very drastic. I never said no to this, but I had to work it through in my heart. My heart was so much with the Mozambican ministry. The mission team pointed out that I had a preaching gift and quite a network of supporters throughout America. Perhaps we should try and work with this and use this time to inspire others in Kingdom mission.

So in 2011, I established the pattern of staying in Mozambique six months and America six months. I'm of retirement age now, but I'm still full of energy! At the beginning of each home furlough, I always stay in Goshen, having a bit of a slower schedule and a little bit of recuperation. That has been so good. Invitations come in to preach around the country, and I preach within my own church as well.

The ministry in Mozambique has adapted to this change. It brings me back to my original thoughts: teach, equip, empower, release. It is time for me to leave much of the day to day running of the ministry, particularly with the orphans, to my Mozambican brothers and sisters. Everything is delegated. Though at first, this was hard for me to adapt to, I can now see that it was also God's tender love and care for me—as I advance in years—that I would not have allowed myself because it's hard for me to slow down.

I've always seen God's hand working out His plans for me and giving me protection, but it was mightily demonstrated in 2012 during my six-month stay in Mozambique when my home was attacked by a gang of robbers. It had been attacked three times before, but this fourth attack left me, the children, and the widow in my home fearing for our lives. For over a year, we had had a wall on three sides of our property with the fourth boundary marked by a thorn bush hedge. To improve security, we had begun to clear this hedge and build a fourth wall, but at that time it was only two cement blocks high.

Two guards stay awake all through the night to protect our property, but I knew we were vulnerable while this building work was taking place. I said to one of the guards, "Please, that hedge is down, and this is a very open space. Please guard it while the other one sits in front." So each night, they did that. But two guards are no match for an armed gang.

The guards, Brother Soza and Brother Antonio, later told me that perhaps 13 or 15 men surrounded and attacked our property. One of them asked, "Where is the Brazilian missionary?" thinking I was Brazilian. Brother Soza replied, "She's not here; she's in Beira." Of course I was sleeping in the house, but he said this to protect me. Then they tried to bind him. Mozambican thieves bind you right away and stuff your mouth with cotton or something, so that you can't shout for help. As they were doing this, Brother Soza must have gotten panicky, seeing the weapons that they were holding (hatchets, metal rods, and guns). He tried to fight himself loose and run away. That's when they attacked him, striking him at least three or four times and chopping his ear in half. He stumbled away in the darkness and fell unconscious.

I woke to voices outside my window, "We are here to kill. We are here to kill." I knew this was to get me to cry out in fear and reveal where I was, so I kept as quiet as I could. The thieves approached the other guard, Brother Antonio, "Where is the missionary?" He said, "She's not here; I don't know where she is." He also knew I was in my bedroom but said this to protect me. They bound him, but he didn't fight it. They held him at gunpoint as the robbery progressed. They hit him in the head once, but he was not severely injured, thank God.

The thieves smashed the lights outside our boys' dormitory. The boys kept quiet, no doubt fearing for their lives. The thieves took 20 minutes to smash through three iron security doors and eight large padlocks into the house. After breaking into the kitchen, they moved into the corridor to the rooms where our widow, Paulina, and the children sleep. They said to Paulina, a very strong woman of faith, "Give us your money; give us your cell phone," and hit her in the face. She gave her money, but she didn't give her cell phone, which was hidden under her mattress. The children huddled under the beds, scared to bits. Our bricklayer was staying in the guest room; he managed to hide in a big cupboard and was not found.

The door into my living area was locked, but the thieves bashed it open and came into my living room and office area. I was two more doors away, shivering in my bedroom, my tongue cleaving to the roof of my mouth. I shook in terror and knelt on the floor with my face on my mattress, and I cried out to the Lord. I had my cell phone with me and called a local policeman, a strong Christian. He had previously told me to call him anytime I needed help, but his line was busy.

I could hear the thieves breaking open my desk drawer, which was locked, and I heard them say, "Bora," which means "Oh, my." They had found the money I had set aside for that month's food, water, and electricity, all used for the general care of the orphans on the compound. They started to break the lock to my guest bedroom, one door away from my bedroom. I managed to call Pastor Rego, who was away at our farmland. He had heard what was happening and was surprised that the police hadn't come yet. They had already been called but went to Pastor Rego's home by mistake.

The thieves got through the guest bedroom door. One door remained into my bedroom, and it was not strong. You never know what you will do in such a situation until you are faced with it. I just cried into my mattress and prayed for protection. I knew it was my only hope. Suddenly, it went totally quiet. They didn't even try my door. I know that God had stationed an angel there. They had found the money, two laptops, and a brand new DVD player I had bought for the children to watch movies. They had decided that was good enough and left. The police arrived with Zitu, Pastor Rego's son. Paulina came to my door, saying, "Mama, you can come out now." We wept in each other's arms, so thankful that we and the children had not been hurt.

Morning dawned, and the neighbors came. They had seen what was going on and felt so bad. I was in shock but at peace. Jesus said, "I will never leave you," and I was so happy that I was alive. I felt so protected. The horror of the situation only entered into my thoughts little by little at first. We found, Brother Soza badly injured but, incredibly, still alive. He took time to recover, suffering permanent hearing loss where they had cut his ear with such force. However, he was brave enough to return to work as a guard for me, for which I am so thankful.

In the days that followed, I felt carried by people's love and compassion. That morning, my Mozambican brothers and sisters, with the church leaders, walked over to my home after church. I knelt with Paulina in front of them, and they prayed for us and sang songs of God's comfort. Some of them cried with us. Over all these years, I have never felt such love and security from my Mozambican brethren; they were like angels unawares for me. It was such a comfort to know that I was not alone.

Over the next couple of days, students from the Bible school which was in session at that time slept outside my house, praying and fasting for our safety and protection. One or two missionaries came, offering prayer and practical support. I spoke with Pastor Steve from my home church, and he prayed with me over the phone. He strongly advised I stay elsewhere for the time being, and my Mozambican brothers and sisters felt the same way. So, once again I moved into a little room in Pastor and Mama Rego's home at their compound. For days, I listened to and was comforted by wonderful Scripture songs assuring me of God's protection and presence in times of trouble.

The shock was still with me, and every time a dog barked, I woke up, wondering if the thieves were returning. For two weeks, I slept lightly, the fear of this event still very much with me. I don't think those thieves wanted to kill me, but if that is what they had to do to get what they wanted, then they probably would have. I looked to the Lord. Whenever the memories and fear of the horror tried to torment me, distract my mind, or cause me not to sleep, I remembered the verse that that I put to music in Israel when I broke my ankle:

"I trust in You, O Lord; I say 'You are my God. My times are in Your hand'" (Psalm 31:15).

A ministry trip to Malawi and our annual pastors' conference was scheduled for just two weeks away. I didn't want the trauma from the theft to stop it. I knew that was Satan's plan. So we carried on with our plans and left for Malawi, meeting up with Reuven and Yanit Ross and Charleeda Sprinkle at Malawi's airport. I usually minister to the children on our ministry trips, and Pastor Rego and our other pastors oversee the meetings with the adults. Over 300 children got saved! That encouraged me so much and was healing to my soul.

There were hundreds of people there, and there was such an anointing and presence of the Holy Spirit as we worshipped the Lord, prayed, and cried out to the Lord. Many had been prayed for—for healings, deliverance, and just for a closer walk with Jesus. As communion was served, Yanit came over to me and said, "I want to break off the trauma of what you've gone through." She prayed for me, and I feel that sealed it, taking away from me the trauma and fear.

As I wrote the first email home after the theft, God reminded me of His words to me, "Tanneken, will you follow Me, come what may?" I answered again, "Yes, Lord, come what may." Even with this horrific experience, He protected me. Later on, I asked the Lord to teach me through this experience, and in my devotions, Psalm 46 came to mind; He reminded me that He is indeed "a very present help in trouble."

I continued to live with the Regos until I left for my six months in America. While I was gone, it was decided that the wall not only needed to be completed but razor wire needed to be placed on top of it all the way around. In all, over $6,000 was raised for this project—once again, a loving gesture from faithful supporters. The work was completed just before I returned in 2013. It was another year in Mozambique. He had more for me to do.

## Mama Paulina, widow and faithful worker in the orphan ministry

When the thieves came to my window, they said, "Today we are not playing a game; today we are here to kill." My hope was to open the office door so that I could get to Mama Tanneken's bedroom. But the office door was locked so it was not possible to get to her. After they had broken the entry door which had five locks, I heard them say to the guard: "Where is the missionary? Where is her car?" Soza, the guard, said "She does not live here; she lives in Beira."

The thieves entered our home and came to my room. They bashed my door open and four thieves came in. Laura and Rainha, the two younger orphan girls, were hiding under my bed, of course very afraid, but they did not cry out. I sat on my bed and the thieves demanded, "Give us your money." I said that I have no money. They hit me two times in the face. Then they demanded that I give my cell phone, but I told them I did not have one. One of them took a katana, a machete, and raised it over my head, wanting to hit me. They said, "Give me your money. If you don't I will cut your head with this machete." I had some money under my pillow and I gave him that. When they broke open the office door and entered, I did not hear Mama Tanneken so I thought they had killed her.

After they had stolen the things, they left. The police arrived with Zito, Pastor Rego's son. Zito called out: "Where is Mama Tanneken?" I said "I do not know; maybe she is in her room." We started to call: "Mama, Mama" and she responded, "I am here." Mama was afraid to come out of her room but we told her that the thieves had gone. When Mama Tanneken came out of her room, she fell into my arms and we just held each other, crying, saying, "Thank you God. You have protected us."

# Farming for Orphans in Mozambique

*If you extend your soul to the hungry and satisfy the
afflicted soul, then your light shall dawn in the darkness,
and your darkness shall be as the noonday.*
Isaiah 58:10

In providing for our children, food, of course, is the greatest need. We provide a very basic diet of mainly corn and dried beans. The hard kernels of corn are beaten down into fine corn flour with huge wooden pestles in a large, deep mortar. Our children, even around age five, do this, two together lifting the pestles up and down over their heads; one raises the pestle up while the other pounds it down onto the corn in the mortar, often singing as they work. This flour is used to make corn mush, cooked in large metal pots over a wood fire. The mush is the consistency of grits or hot cereal, but at our compound, there's no milk, sugar, or seasoning added. They eat this with the beans.

Though the markets are full of vegetables, fruits, chickens and fish, they are often too expensive for our budget. There's no candy, cookies, or cokes. When a ladies' Sunday School group heard of the children's needs, they made it a monthly project to raise enough money for every child to have a cup of milk and one bread roll every Sunday. On special occasions we were able to give the children a treat, a meal with rice, fish, chicken and a bottle of Coke.

We've tried raising chickens and ducks for eggs but it hasn't been successful. We've also taught the children how to grow things in a garden, but garden space is very limited. Then I first crossed paths with Janet Phythian from England and her daughter Gabriella. We were at a Resurrection Sunday sunrise service on the Indian Ocean led by Beira International Fellowship, a small ever-changing group of internationals, many of whom were fellow missionaries. I sat next to Janet at the breakfast that followed, and after greeting each other, we started talking. I told her about our orphan ministry and something of the struggle to feed the children, but how God had always provided enough, day by day.

I learned that Janet had established a 200-hectare (494-acre) farm further inland from Dondo where she had a community enterprise growing organic tea tree oil. She had lived for nine years in Mozambique, but had now moved back to England. She returned each year to oversee her farm. During her time in Mozambique, she had become a Christian. She shared with me how God had spoken to her about dedicating part of the land for orphans or the poor to develop agriculture.

I am never very shy about asking for help. Just knock at the door! I asked Janet if she would consider our ministry. Our kids' diet needed more of a variety of vegetables and fruit. Janet visited us and agreed to see what she could do. At first, she gave us five low-lying acres for rice. The first year was not productive, because there was no rain. We had prepared the land late in the season. In the second year, we grew our first little bit of rice; and then the third year more rain came. That was the first good year. This small variation in the children's diet was such a blessing.

*The woman with blond hair and a white blouse is Janet Phythian. The name of her business is Africa Naturally and her mission is Farming for Orphans in Mozambique. She is showing Mama Rego, some of the orphans and me how to grow vegetables, rice and banana trees using the Farming-God's-Way approach.*

*That's me shopping at the fish market in Beira, buying fish for the orphans.*

Janet has then encouraged us in a wider agricultural project using principles of the biblically-based Foundations for Farming[1] using techniques such as crop rotation, avoiding turning the soil, and leaving land fallow to recover its nutrients. Dead leaves are used to cover tender new shoots, and these leaves rot down into the soil, enriching it to encourage new growth. These principles are not widely practiced here in Mozambique. Janet agreed to train three in our church, two men and one woman, in the Foundations for Farming techniques and to grow vegetables to contribute to the children's diet. This started in 2013, with our trainees growing tomatoes, onions, cabbage, beetroot and carrots, and these went into the children's diets. This was a small start, but in time, we hope we will see our children getting more vitamins and minerals through these precious veggies. Yes! They are truly "precious" to us! Recently too we've been able to give the children fish every week.

She has also introduced us to the moringa tree; its leaves and seeds are very nutritious. I had one tree planted in my yard, and after a couple of years, we took 20 saplings from it. It is very easy to plant, so the older children do it. They just cut up the branches into around 24-inch pieces and stick them in the ground and water them. They grow very fast and once they produce leaves, the leaves are harvested, ground fine and added to any food. They grow so fast that we can harvest these leaves a few times a year. Since we can't afford to buy the children vitamins, this is a wonderful alternative.

Janet is always keen to move things on, and she hopes next to grow beans. With her support, our trainees have also planted 100 banana saplings for the orphan project so that in a couple of years, we will have a plentiful supply of bananas. Foundations for Farming puts God at the center of this mission, and her farm manager leads Bible studies with our trainees each morning before work begins. We hope that the people Janet and her team train will use the Foundational Farming principles in their own small plots or in kitchen gardens and pass on their skills to others.

When you take up God's call, God puts the right people in your life. He's the one that gives you those links to make His vision in a ministry possible. Janet is but one example. God has given me many other Christian brothers and sisters who have come alongside me, an incredible network of partners who have made this journey a joy.

## From Janet Phythian
## Farming for Orphans in Mozambique

God had been speaking to me, saying there was a mission in Mozambique that He wanted me to help. My daughter and I met Tanneken at that sunrise service. I don't know why I told her and nobody else that God had been speaking to me in this way. Tanneken seemed very certain it was her church's orphan ministry God was talking about. She was very compelling. How could I refuse to visit? We went to visit the children and from there agreed to help, using the principles of Foundations for Farming.

When you are teaching Foundations for Farming, God is right there in the centre, because it teaches four principles for farming that you can transfer into your life. Firstly, doing things on time. There is no point in planting your lettuces in Mozambique in July. It's too hot; they will just not grow. Secondly, doing things with quality. You must be careful how you prepare the land, without using ploughing or chemical additives that destroy the nutrient build up in the soil. If you leave it, you produce this wonderful microbial activity in the soil that is what the plants need and what the soil needs to be the best that it can be. The third principle is no wastage; you take care not to waste any of the vegetation around you, which is part of God's precious creation, but to use it to naturally enrich the soil.

Then comes the fourth principle, doing things with joy. The joy comes; God gives us joy. It's hard work in Mozambique in the farming areas that we are talking about. It's hard work, but it's God's work. We are feeding ourselves, we are feeding others, and we can do it with joy because we know that God is right there with us. We are honouring Him in everything we are doing in the farming. There is a synergy with the church and the orphan ministry, with growing people for God.

I had my very close team who have been working together for years on the farm, and then we interjected these three people from Mountain of Praise Church. It could have all gone horribly wrong. What happens now is that every morning they have a Bible study and they pray for each other, which is just fantastic. That had never happened before. There are several people that work for the tea tree oil enterprise that don't go to church or call themselves Christians, even one Muslim lady; they all pray together to God at the beginning of the day.

In the first year of vegetable growing, we started growing in April and by the end of August, we had produced over 600kg [1,322 lbs] of vegetables. With lots of children, it's not a large amount for each child each day, but it's a good result for the first year, and God was right there in that.

The trainees I think have learned a great deal about the farming, and they have really come together as a team. There are things they have talked about in their Bible studies that I am sure they have heard before in church, but hearing it in the context of their daily life has brought it alive. It was almost like a big surprise that in the daily watering, God is with them. We all agreed they could pray as they were walking up and down. I think their eyes were opened a lot to the message that God is right there with them all the time.

It's a bit like when Jesus was here. He used to meet people where they were. He didn't say, I'm standing in the synagogue or wherever, you come to Me. He actually went to people, and I think His parables were things they would understand. It's a bit like that; we're using the agriculture because people need food and if more and more families can grow it, there will be better nutrition for everybody. That's quite a big hope for growing it, to have as many families as possible growing vegetables through these principles. Yet, also it's a mission like any other where people learn more about God, where people are brought closer to God. We hope that one of the three trainees will want to support others in Dondo in farming this way.

I am part of the '4 O'Clock Service' of St. Nicholas Church in Sevenoaks, England. The leadership of this congregation agreed they wanted to be more outward focussed and support three overseas ministries. Our larger church has many such links, but our congregation was just getting started in this. They chose my link to support the farming mission alongside Tanneken's church's orphan ministry. Many people now support and pray for our mission. Some of our young people have gone out on short term mission in their gap years, helping Tanneken and the church in the orphan ministry.

Out of that, St. Boswell's Primary School, a Church of England school that is attached to our church, has been supporting us in a huge way. Their older children, aged 10 to 11, have a worship council, which has grown from 6 to 20 or more. One of our church family meets with them every week. They pray and do activities in the school that highlight what is going on in Mozambique. I am given a slot in an assembly once a term to update and inspire the children.

What we are doing now isn't the end of it. We hope that the vegetable growing can take place nearer to the orphan ministry. Ideas are being put in our hearts, ideas for the orphans that are beginning to finish school and going into a situation where there aren't many jobs. Alongside improved farming methods, there seems a lot of possibilities for the start of mini-enterprises. We are so overwhelmed with the abundance of the harvest and how smoothly everything went this last 12 months [2014]. That's not down to us; God has paved the way.

# Worth It All

*Assuredly, I say to you, there is no one who has left
house or brothers or sisters or father or mother or wife
or children or lands, for My sake and the gospel's, who
shall not receive a hundredfold now in this time—houses
and brothers and sisters and mothers and children and
lands, with persecutions—and in the age to come eternal
life. But many who are first will be last, and the last first.*
Mark 10:29-31

Jesus' promise in Mark has strengthened and encouraged me many times in my 25 years of missions. I have learned and am still learning to trust and obey, come what may. In all these years, God has been so faithful, so loving, so merciful, and truly a Refuge and Shelter in good and difficult times. I thank the Lord for all who have made and are continuing to make this journey in Kingdom mission with me.

Foremost is my home church, Harvest Community Church, who are truly family to me. Their encouragements, prayers, and financial help have played a major part ever since I was sent out by them. Over the years, they have provided two trucks, property and a house, monthly support, and various teams. Pastor Steve and Ronda Chupp have made me feel very welcome from the time that I made Harvest Community my home church until today. They helped and encouraged me to find the calling God had on my life in evangelism, international missions, the founding of Mountain of Praise Church, and its church family-based orphan care ministry. When the expanding network of Mountain of Praise churches and the orphan ministry needed more structure, they set up an advocate team and a board of directors.

Ronda has been a spiritual mother to me. Many years ago, God spoke to me through a dream concerning her. I was walking by myself and then she appeared in the dream. I stretched my hand out to her and said to her, "God says that you should be my spiritual guide and mother." I shared this with Ronda and thank the Lord for her kind, sisterly, and loving concern she has shown all these years. Even though I had my big family in Mozambique, it is a gift for us single missionaries to have the church as family.

Missions Directors Tim and Joan Morningstar have encouraged, advised, and helped me in countless ways. Their annual visits to Mozambique and guidance with donations, accounting, and forming the TCF Mercy non-profit incorporation have been an invaluable gift to me.

Since 2003, I live six months of each year in Mozambique and six months in the US. The six months in America have given me time to nurture other partnerships. One such connection has developed with Reno Presbyterian Church in Nevada. A member there, Giesela Wegner, grew up with me in Paraguay and made contact with me again after reading Rolland and Heidi Baker's book, *Always Enough.* I went to speak at their church, and they asked to adopt me as their missionary. This has been such a blessing and encouragement. Since then, I visit this church in the Sierra Mountains every year and speak at the church, to the ladies' Bible study, the youth, and the children's church. They have helped provide a truck, finish the security wall around my house, and sent a team that put a roof on the boy's dorm and built bunk beds. Among that same team was Cassie Hemsley, filming and interviewing the leaders and youth of Mountain of Praise Church. She has produced two lovely videos which aid me as I preach and share in my partner churches..

A similar relationship has formed with Tyler Trinity Lutheran Church in Tyler, Texas. Joan Rappleyea and I reconnected after having met at St. Paul's Lutheran church in Albany, New York over 30 years ago. Today we thankfully receive monthly gifts for the child sponsorship and nursery school program.

God has also made connections for me in England, firstly of course with Janet Phythian and her program of Farming for Orphans in Mozambique as I described earlier. Unexpectedly I formed a link with Müllers, the present day organisation founded by George Müller in the 19th century. This mission to orphans 150 years ago has always been an inspiration to me, so on a visit to Bristol, England, to visit my dear author Maria, I was surprised to learn that Müller's work continues today. Maria showed me the old orphan houses in Bristol, now turned

*My brother Hänsel (Hans) and his wife Vera have encouraged and helped me over many years in mission work in Mozambique.*

*My brother Melchior (Mel) and his wife Janet have continued to be family for me and have generously supported my work in Mozambique.*

into a college and flats, but still solidly standing as a witness of God's faithful provision.

They have widened their ministry to "Orphans of the World" and help to support and channel support to many orphan projects and missionaries throughout the poorer regions of the globe.[2] As George Müller began, by faith they pray for all their needs and wait for the Lord to provide. A trustee, Ed Marsh, met with me, and they agreed to include us in their daily prayers, sharing our news with their prayer network. To have the support and prayers of this historic Christian organization is something I could not have imagined. It is like God is showing me His plans will continue even when my own efforts have ceased.

As wonderful as all these friendships have been, I have continually longed for a renewal of friendship with my natural family, especially with my three sisters and my mother who were living in the Bruderhof communities. I am so thankful to my brothers Hans and Mel and their families who have been so loving, supportive, and helpful. It was a joy for me to have family to go to, especially on the holidays like Christmas and Easter.

As I've noted before, Hans and Vera have come to Mozambique twice to help with building projects. Mel and Janet have supported the orphan work generously and have helped in other ways. Even though Mel has been deaf since 1967, he is still singing all the songs he remembers from his childhood and teen years in the community. He can no longer sing in tune, but that is no hindrance to him or to me. When I visit Mel and Janet at Christmas time, one of our best moments is singing the beloved German and English Christmas carols together. But I still prayed for and yearned for greater contact and renewed relationship and friendship with the rest of my Fros family and the Bruderhof community that they are part of. Praise God, the Lord saw the desire of my heart and graciously arranged it.

For over 30 years, I had minimal contact with my mother, my three sisters or any other members of the community of my childhood, the Bruderhof. When my mother was very old, I visited her and my sisters who were all in

*2005: Mother and I are celebrating my 60th birthday.*

one of the Bruderhof communities in England. We met at a restaurant, and we were able to embrace and kiss each other. It was so healing. As it was Christmas, they brought decorations and candles and made a beautiful table there in the restaurant and ordered a wonderful meal. At the end, they gave me a gift and even sang "Happy Birthday" to me, given I was born shortly after Christmas.

As it was time to leave, my three sisters and brother-in-law needed to get my mother into her wheelchair and back into the car. They all went out, and I was alone with her. I asked if she remembered the prayer she sang to us at our bedside as children. Mother remembered the song very well, and so I held her hands as we sang it together in German:

> I am tired and I will go to rest, I close my eyes;
> Father, let your eyes watch over me.
> If I have done wrong today, dear God, do not hold
>     this against me.
> Your grace and the blood of Jesus forgives all wrong.

Being able to sing this song with mother in her old age was for me the most precious moment of all my life with Mama, who I did not see again before she died.

I had always prayed to God for renewed contact with the community. Some years later, I felt God answered me and said, "Be a spiritual bridge builder." In prayer, I asked the Lord how and with whom shall I do this. He answered, "Start with the Bruderhof community." I wrote to the elders of the communities, and they responded kindly.

*In 2005 I celebrated my 60th birthday with my family at a restaurant in Canterbury, England. Seated from left: Mother, me, Klaus, Irene, Susi-Lucia and Mechthild (standing).*

*Lenora is playing with the orphans on a hot day.*

A visit was arranged, and I was received with love and grace at the Maple Ridge community close to Kingston, New York. I shared with the guest wardens about the ministry to orphans. They were very interested and receptive of all that I shared of God's work among the many orphans, widows, and the poorest of the poor in Mozambique.

From times past, I knew that the Bruderhof sent young people to voluntary service either in the US or other countries. I was bold enough to ask if they would consider sending us some volunteers. From this request came the six-month visit to Mozambique of Lenora, a dear 18-year-old teen, who helped us so much in the care of the orphans, teaching English and teaching the older teens to play the guitar.

Lenora was with me when I became very ill with malaria. I have had this illness four times, but this time, I was so unwell that I could not even stand. Along with my Mozambican sisters, Lenora showed incredible care and patience, a maturity beyond her years.

During Lenora's time with me, I began to receive a few kind notes from my sisters, expressing appreciation that Lenora could be with me. After she returned, Lenora's parents expressed much appreciation that their daughter could be with us, and that she had changed so much during the time with us. I thank the Lord for all that He worked in our hearts, so that not only a spiritual bridge was built, but that this opened the door to future visits to see my sisters, nieces and nephews and greet many, many brothers and sisters that I knew so well. Much love and joy was expressed from both sides. On one of my later visits, one brother expressed it this way: "Thank you, Tanneken, for doing Kingdom mission for us." That brought much inner healing without many words. I am thankful for the friendship I have with the community of my birth and their kind support of me and the orphan ministry.

I cannot bring my story to an end without reflecting on the gift of family in Dondo, Mozambique—especially Pastor Rego and his wife, Cicilia—and our God-given vision for orphan care, evangelism and church planting. While still living at Pastor Rego's, I awoke one morning to hear our youngest orphans playing "church." At the top of their voices, they shouted "Hallelujah!" many times, just like we do often at the beginning of a church service. When I see our little ones—who were rescued from very difficult situations, even close to death through hunger and disease—shouting "Hallelujah," I think, it's worth it all. When I see the children walk to school every day in their uniforms; when I hear some of our youth who have been raised with us say they want to be a doctor, teacher, architect, artist, music teacher, or engineer; when I hear all the children gathered at night for their evening prayers, singing so beautifully to Jesus and praying for God's protection, I know it's worth it all.

When I am privileged to be part of Mountain of Praise Church in its authentic Mozambican way of worship; when I receive the kind protection, care and sense of family from Pastor Rego and his wife Cicilia; when I hear the exhortations to become true followers of Jesus; when government officials, soldiers, witch doctors, and sorcerers convert to Christ; it is worth it all. When we are privileged to hold

*The orphans are praying in the first small MOP church building next to Pastor Rego's home.*

a Bible school and conference to equip and train leaders for godly character in Kingdom living; when I see the nationals preach the Gospel and plant more and more churches in Mozambique and into Malawi and Zimbabwe; when government officials turn to pastors to ask for prayer, acknowledging that God's power comes through prayer, I know that it is worth it all.

When over 2,000,000 World Missionary Press Scripture booklets have been distributed and eagerly received, including areas where the Word of God has not yet entered; when we are able to pray for the sick and dying in the Beira Central Hospital and sense their appreciation of being comforted by prayer and receiving the Word of God, it is worth it all. When we are privileged to be given an outpouring of God's compassion, love and mercy among the poorest of the poor; when I see the Holy Spirit's power of deliverance and healing, then I know it is worth is all. Jesus' love, grace, mercy, compassion and forgiveness of sin are for us all. It is a privilege, joy, and great gift to be part of spreading God's love and salvation in Jesus with a people group that has faced, and continues to face, many difficulties and extreme poverty. Yes, it is worth it all!

# Lessons Learned

*Assuredly, I say to you, inasmuch as you did it to one of the
least of these My brethren, you did it to Me.*
Matthew 25:40

After having experienced 25 years of Christian service and mission, I can only testify that this never came about by my personal plan or design, but by God's great love and divine purpose for my life. I am a person just like everyone else, but I have tried to obey God's calling—without knowing where it would take me. I thank my Lord for an exciting, and at times, challenging life journey. I did not know that it was the Lord's voice in 1965 that said, "Tanneken, will you follow Me, come what may?" But Jesus revealed Himself to me and guided me over and over again through His Word, His holy Presence, His giving of visions, and the wisdom of others. In His faithfulness, He never abandoned me.

After recuperating from knee replacement surgery in 2015, the Lord spoke to me. He gently said, "I am restoring you, inwardly and physically, so that I can send you forth once more to help serve others with the love of God and salvation in Jesus Christ." Therefore, at 69 years of life, I continued to follow the Lord's heart to rescue the orphans, comfort the widows, the poor, the handicapped, the lonely, the outcasts, the dying, and ones in despair.

All the victories, the supernatural miracles and deliverances, the rescued children, the hardships, disappointments, the life-threatening moments and serious illnesses—even my own failures and weaknesses—fade because I know my Lord Jesus has guided, carried, protected and equipped me for what He has purposed me to do on this earth.

I leave you, dear reader, with a few thoughts about the lessons I have learned over the years. I pray they will help you as you consider your part in the wonderful work of the Kingdom.

**1.** My first and most important lesson to be learned was that in order to follow Jesus and do the good works He has planned for me to do, I needed to believe and accept Jesus Christ as my personal Lord and Savior. I was enlightened and guided by the assuring words out of Ephesians 2:8-10.

> "For it is by grace you have been saved through faith, and that not of yourselves, it is the gift of God, not of works, lest anyone should boast. For we are His workmanship, created in Christ Jesus for good works, which God prepared beforehand that we should walk in them."

**2.** Listen to the Lord's voice and call for your life. Seek direction and get strengthened through God's wonderful, guiding, never-failing Word; get confirmation from trusted men and women of God.

**3.** Don't choose the easy way out, the people-pleasing way out; don't choose the comfortable or the familiar way. Be courageous! Trust the Lord! Fight the paralyzing effect of fear of the unknown or leaving a comfortable lifestyle. Jesus left heaven's glory to come to our sin-torn world. The Lord will equip and enable you for what He has called you to do.

**4.** Be a pioneer in Kingdom missions, or help someone be a pioneer. If you cannot be the "sent one," be a sender and support others as they reach out. Both roles are part of God's purposes.

**5.** Don't try to have all the plans and provisions made before you obey God's call. Trust and obey the Lord. He will guide and provide!

**6.** Listen to the Lord's voice and follow Him, wherever He leads you. Humble yourself in the sight of the Lord.

**7.** Come humbly to the people God sends you to. Don't come with "I know it all" or "I am better" attitude. Walk humbly with your God and with your neighbor. In cross-cultural missions, do not try to change a nation, a culture, or a people group. Remember Paul's advice in 1 Corinthians 9:19-23: "For though I am free from all men, I have made myself a servant to all, that I might win the more...I have become all things to all men, that I might by all means save some."

**8.** Be brave and uncompromising in the truth of the Gospel.

**9.** Always keep Jesus first with God's Kingdom as your vision and goal. Die to selfish ambitions and "we are used to doing it this way" thoughts or arguments; be flexible and available.

**10.** Keep short accounts. Forgive quickly, even before someone says "I am sorry;" Jesus did that for you and me. Do not remember or repeat other people's sins. God does not do that.

**11.** Do not "gossip" about other people's sin in your churches or on the Internet; we will give an account for everything we say, think, and do. Only pray for the person's repentance and coming back to God the Father whose arms are open wide to receive a repentant person. Jesus did that with the woman caught in adultery and teaches us the same in Matthew 18:15-20.

**12.** Allow the Lord to chisel, shape and mold you for Kingdom missions, and you will bear much fruit for His glory. Knowing and believing that all authority in heaven and on earth has been given to Jesus, go and make disciples of all nations. If you can't go physically, help others to go through your prayers, financial gifts, and encouragements.

**13.** Don't give up or run away when the going is tough; that's the time when the Lord needs you. By His Presence and promises, He helps you to persevere, be it through hardships, persecution, war, sickness, false accusations or personal attack. God's power and glory will be revealed through you as you are faithful.

**14.** Do not build your own "kingdom" in mission; pray with and work in cooperation with other ministries. Do not have a competitive spirit that wants to be known more than other ministries. Trust God for the increase.

**15.** Don't try to run the ministry yourself or rule over the nationals in whose country you are a guest. Serve by working side by side with the nationals of that country. Pray and seek the Lord's guidance together so that they are part of the decision making and giving of ideas in all aspects of the mission. Delegate, teach, equip, empower, and release. Let people flow in their gifting and calling. As we recognize the orphans' giftings, we see many of them grow into confident youth who are leading in worship and prayer, preaching the Word, and helping in the Sunday school and orphan care programs.

To all of you who have walked with me in this adventurous journey—embracing the orphans, the widows, and the lost among the poorest of the poor—and to you who hear the call from the Lord to follow Him wherever He leads you, be strengthened, assured, and comforted by Jesus' timeless invitation:

> **Come, you blessed of My Father, inherit the kingdom prepared for you from the foundation of the world; for I was hungry and you gave Me food; I was thirsty and you gave Me drink; I was a stranger and you took Me in; I was naked and you clothed Me; I was sick and you visited Me; I was in prison and you came to Me...Assuredly, I say to you, inasmuch as you did it to one of the least of these My brethren, you did it to Me.** Matthew 25:34-36, 40

I pray, dear reader that you hear the Lord's call upon your life, that your heart breaks for what breaks His, and that you step out in faith on the exciting road He has ahead of you. Hallelujah!

# Appendix

## Life Story of Pastor António Rego Dias

I, António Rego Dias, was born on 01 of January 1956, son of António Rego Dias and Carlota Tomo, from the district of Marromeu, the Administrative post of Chupanga-Lacerdonia, province of Sofala in Mozambique.

Two years after I was born, my father began to get sick and he called all his family to declare my name, as all his other children were girls. Before the whole family, my father declared and decided that "he would die so his son would live" and "from this day on my son will be called by my name (António)." A few days later, he became very sick. At the point of death, he requested the presence of all my older sisters with his two wives—I was the son of the younger wife. I had five sisters. I am writing this with tears falling, but I need to leave my story and to encourage other orphans and widows.

Imagine my father, lying on a reed mat. I went to sit by him and he took me with both his hands so I could sleep on his stomach. Shortly after he left this world. He died and I was taken off him. The next day he was buried at midnight, with only his family around him. He was buried in our garden, where we would throw the rubbish after sweeping our house. It was like this that misfortune fell on us. We lived with our uncle, my parent's youngest son.

We began to suffer, and it was so bad that my sisters left to go to their mother's house. I continued to live with my uncle with all the suffering of nudity, hunger – the living conditions were difficult. I didn't have shorts or a t-shirt. I just used a white cloth, which was also used as a blanket, my mat and for when I went out. I began to study with a lot of difficulty, always using the cloth. I had shoes made from the skins of the plants of the banana trees, and I made a hat from the leaves of the banana tree to protect me from the sun when I went to school. After school, I began to often go to the Catholic church and the priest eventually asked my uncle if I could accompany him, teaching the word of God in the community.

When I was 12, God began to use me through dreams and visions. He used me so greatly that people were even able to escape from their situations through my dreams. But those who did not follow my advice suffered. There was great suffering during the colonial times. Police came to our communities searching for people who didn't pay taxes, recruiting for the army, for forced labour, to work in the manufacturing of alcoholic drinks, and [through visions] I could alert the community by foreshadowing the future.

When I was 16, I left school because I was limited with how to continue with my studies. I didn't stop learning; I learnt how to drive a Caterpillar truck. It was then that I began to recover and knew what a shirt, shorts and sandals were.

I always continued to pray strongly. Sometimes we went fishing, spending the night on an island surrounded by the Zambezi River. Once a hippopotamus came and caused my brothers to flee, forcefully separating the ashes of our campfire, but he let me sleep and nothing bad happened to me. Twice, my uncle sent me away from his home. As I was looking for a place to sleep, I crossed paths with a hyena.

I ended up joining the army in the war of liberation of Mozambique. I never stopped praying at the base until one day the commander surprised me as I was praying underneath a tree. The commander got very angry with me and took all the books I used for prayer and burnt them. From then on I prayed in my heart during the ten years of the war for independence.

I felt a strong urge to leave the army but for two years I was scared of telling the most superior commander. During that time I was functioning as the Political Commissioner. One morning I found the courage to speak to the commander. I approached him and said that I wanted to leave the quarters and return home. The commander immediately dispensed me, and that was how I left the military life. I arrived in Dondo; I couldn't return to my place of birth—the district of Marromeu—but Dondo was also in the province of Sofala so I stayed there. For six years I didn't go to church.

One day in October I felt a very strong calling to start praying again at the Pentecostal church. So on one Sunday I decided to look for a church. My wife and I walked from seven in the morning until two in the afternoon. We saw many churches but we did not enter them.

We became tired, so we decided to return home. Following the idea to return home, I began to feel pains in my stomach and I entered into the bush and had severe diarrhea with much blood. I began to lose my strength straight away. Two more times I lost blood in the same way, and the time arrived when I couldn't walk anymore.

I sat on the ground and sent my wife to look for one of the churches to help me. After a few minutes, I felt I should enter the Assembly of God church, and the minute I thought that, I felt cured and so I called my wife to return. I stood up and we walked directly to this church. It was four in the afternoon. The leaders were in the church and I asked to be converted. This was the church of Pastor Bizeque, who discipled me and later on became part of Mountain of Praise Church.

Three months passed and God began to give me visions until the fourth month where I felt a very strong urge to preach, so that even as I walked I would preach to the grass in silence. The day that God moved the pastor of the church to let me start preaching, God did something marvelous that day.

As soon as I gave my first sermon, God used me with the gifts of healing and deliverance. Demons began to come out of people and others were healed. One Sunday, after leaving church as I sat at home, I saw someone approaching. They had brought a mentally disturbed woman from the Catholic church who needed prayer. When we arrived at her house, I was allowed to enter. I asked her to kneel and I prayed for her. When she had calmed down, I proclaimed prayer and fasting and she was totally healed.

After this miracle we went into the bush way outside the city, walking from five in the morning until six in the evening. When we arrived, we were immediately called to a house where the son was in the central prison, and they were all witchdoctors. I asked them to convert so their son could leave the prison and they accepted. We burnt all the instruments of witchcraft they had and the next day their son was set free from prison. The same afternoon, a mentally disturbed boy appeared. I prayed and he was cured.

After three days, we returned home and spent three days and nights in prayer and fasting, not even drinking water. Then the pastor sent me to pray for a mentally disturbed man who had been ill for four years and he was cured. From this moment, the prayer and fasting was a constant part of my life.

We have known God's protection from wild animals. For six months, every night we heard steps on our roof, but it was never able to enter our house. One afternoon two leopards appeared. My son saw them and called me to see them, and they fled. Another day, very early in the morning, I was going to the bathroom. A leopard was at the hosepipe on my way to the bathroom. Before I saw it, I felt my skin crawling. When I looked on the top of the hosepipe and saw it, I began to pray and the leopard jumped away. After that I began to pray and fast and I received a vision where it appeared I was killing the leopard. After that the leopards vanished and were not heard or seen again.

Four times I have seen the Lord raise people from the dead. First, a mother, who a member of our community knew well, secondly a child of our church. Thirdly a young boy called Zeca, whose mother and family still pray with us now at our church; and finally a Catholic lady called Catija.

Each time the Lord worked in a similar way. After a few minutes in the home, I felt someone telling me that I could pray for this person who had passed away. But I couldn't identify how resurrection would happen. I asked the families if they would give me permission to pray, and they decided that I could. I began with a song of adoration. I immediately felt a reviving of the power of the Lord in my body. After this sign I saw a strong illumination. I knelt at the head of the dead person and I took the cloth off the head of this person and took hold of the head, praying. This was when the Lord brought them back to life.

This gifting stopped but I still saw the Lord healing in miraculous ways and liberating people from demons. After this I went to Bible school in Maputo where God worked a lot.

There were floods, and I helped to distribute food and preach the Word together with foreigners who came with donations. I walked in Maputo and Gaza. On the day we went to Gaza, specifically in the district of Chokwe, where there were 60 000 refugees of the flood, there were many strangers in our car, including Pastor Surpresa, mother Tanneken and me. But when we arrived there, there was heavy rain with loud thunder and we couldn't leave the car.

In the car I heard the voice of God speaking to me: "Rego get out of your car and pray outside." Pastor Surpresa and Mother Tanneken forbade me from leaving the car because the situation outside was bad. With great strength I left the car to pray outside. I prayed and there was a great clap of thunder. The rain stopped, and when we had all gathered in that place, we began to pray with a great strength. Following the miracle of the rain, I was able to preach to the 60,000 people at that camp. It really was a marvelous thing that God made happen. Many were

*Pastor Rego and his wife Cicilia are standing in front of the Mountain of Praise Church in Dondo. They were founders of this indigenous church, together with other Mozambican pastors and me.*

cured and others liberated.

In 2001 I was taken by airplane to the north of the Sofala province to attend the situation of the floods. There were many miracles there as well, in the district of Marromeu, the district where I was born. I stayed there for two months before they came to take me home. On yet another mission I went to Malawi. There I led a conference with 10,000 people in one week. Twice at the pulpit I was challenged by a snake that wanted to bite me. It did not scare me. I preached with strength and the snake was stopped by the power of God and the people killed it.

God always worked in my life. Once I made the trip to preach in the USA and Canada. God showed His glory in my life and used me with great strength amongst those people.

It was then that I was shown a new mission. I explained to Mother Tanneken that when I returned to Mozambique, I would find conflicts. This really happened, and so I decided to leave the ministry of God. At the same time, God communicated with me and with Mother Tanneken to join together to start a new mission in Mozambique. God showed us the way and we started. The response was strong and we began to operate with evangelism. God began to give us many visions. God is good forever for those who love Him. He will always live in them.

God embraces man with all His love. Let's believe in God with all that He is.

Thank you!
António Rego Dias

# Acknowledgements

First, I want to express my deepest appreciation to Maria Stuart, who helped write my biography, for her endless hours, yes months, of researching the "God-stories" that shaped my life story. Her sensitive and Holy Spirit-led way of weaving my life story into a biography is a gift to me, my family and many brothers and sisters in Christ who have walked with me in Kingdom mission for these 26 years. A special thank you goes to Maria's husband Paul and their two children for giving up much of their mother's precious family time as she was writing.

Without the help of my brother Melchior in researching many of the background facts, including his skill of remembering details of our childhood, without the editorial skill of Charleeda Sprinkle, without the designer's gift of Harriet Miller, this book would not be written and assembled the way it is. In addition, a heartfelt thank you to those who will help to publish my life story.

I am thankful for the many years of wise counsel and mentoring of Reuven and Yanit Ross; and the faithful support and help of Pastor Steve and Ronda Chupp and my precious sending church, Harvest Community Church.

Tim and Joan Morningstar have helped me in countless ways: by writing my prayer newsletters, logistics, legalities as a Permanent Resident, accounting, and always encouraging me in my call to missions abroad. I cannot forget the hundreds of brothers, sisters, youth, teens and children in Christ who have encouraged, prayed and given financially to the God-given command to care for orphans, widows, the poor, and to GO and preach the Gospel of Jesus Christ to all nations.

I am so thankful for the friendship, acceptance and respect in the partnership in Kingdom mission with Pastor Rego and his wife Cicilia and all the Mozambican brothers, sisters, youth, teens and children at

Mountain of Praise Church. Without all these dear brothers and sisters in Christ, my life story would not have happened in this way.

But most of all, I give thanks to God, my Father, to Jesus Christ, my Savior, and to the Holy Spirit, my Guide and Empowerer, who day by day fills me with love, mercy, and compassion. I give thanks for His abiding Presence, His embrace and His protection through all of my life.

TO GOD ALONE BE ALL THE GLORY!
HALLELUJAH!

# Endnotes

**Introduction**

(1) *The Hiding Place*, by Corrie Ten Boom with John and Elizabeth Sherrill, Hodder & Stoughton, 1971, p20

**Chapter 1**

(1) *The Martyr's Mirror*, pp. 647-651

**Chapter 2**

(1) *A Joyful Pilgrimage* by Emmy Arnold, Plough Publishing House, 2007.

(2) For a full account of the Bruderhof's stand at this time please see, *An Embassy Besieged*, by Emmy Barth, Cascade Books/Plough Publishing, 2010.

(3) *An Embassy Besieged*, by Emmy Barth, as above.

(4) Renate Olins' account of her Jewish German family's experience has her father being suddenly taken one evening by two British detectives, and not hearing for some months where he was being held. See *What did you do in the War, Mummy?*, by Mavis Nicholson, Chatto & Windus, 1995.

(5) *No Lasting Home*, by Emmy Barth, Plough Publishing House, 2009.

(6) www.bluestarline.org

(7) *No Lasting Home*, by Emmy Barth, as above.

(8) www.mcc.org is the website for the Mennonite Central Committee, which works in development and relief across the world, as the outreach arm of this wide ranging Anabaptist denomination.

(9) In *No Lasting Home* Emmy Barth talks about Tanneken's mother's experience, and describes a most difficult time in the heat and dust of the Chaco. Like other babies born around this time Jan Peter became ill early on, and some died in the early years in Paraguay.

## Chapter 3

(1) A 19th Century child's bedtime prayer written by Luise Hensel , 'I am tired and I will go to rest, Closing my eyes. Father, let your eyes Watch over me. If I have done anything wrong today, dear God, do not hold that against me. Your grace and the blood of Jesus will take away all our failings.' Tanneken's translation.

(2) Child's bedtime prayer by Luise Hensel, as above, Tanneken's translation.

(3) *Amahl and the Night Visitors,* an opera by Gian Carlo Menotti, words of King Melchior as remembered by Melchior Fros.

(4) A carol copied from a worn, stained and handmade songbook with a wooden back, dating from the 40's in Paraguay.

(5) A guampa is a cup made often made from an animal horn, and traditionally used in Paraguay to serve yerba maté, or tereré, a cold drink made from the same plant.

(6) Sweetened condensed milk.

## Chapter 4

(1) Traditional Swiss German carol, origin unknown, translation – Melchior Fros.

(2) Bulstrode Park is now the Headquarters of the mission agency, WEC. www.wec-int.org.uk

## Chapter 6

(1) '*Leave It In The Hands Of The Lord,*' by Sebastian Temple, taken from *Sing Your Praise to God.*

## Chapter 7

(1) *Jonathan Livingston Seagull* by Richard Bach, Grafton Books 1970, p46.

(2) Luke 18:9-14. Publican in this context means a tax collector for the Romans.

(3) 1 Corinthians 11:5 is the key verse that this belief is based upon.

(4) '*Fill my cup*' by Richard E Blanchard.

## Chapter 8

(1) All excerpts from the service taken from a cassette recording of Tanneken's baptism service by her friend Kay.

## Chapter 9

(1) Zion Chapel is now known as Harvest Community Church, www. hccgoshen.org

## Chapter 10

(1) David Davis has written their story in his book *The Road to Carmel*, 1997.

(2) I Corinthians 7:7 talks about singleness and marriage as a gift.

## Chapter 12

(1) Go to www.mullers.org for an account of the work of George Muller and the Foundation's continuing mission today.

## Chapter 13

(1) Rolland and Heidi have written about these experiences in their book, *Always Enough*, Chosen Books, 2003.

(2) Again told by Rolland and Heidi Baker, in *Always Enough*, where Heidi talks of two further occasions where she saw the blind see with Tanneken.

## Chapter 14

(1) *Mozambique and the Great Flood of 2000*, Frances Christie and Joseph Hanlon, The International African Institute, 2001.

(2) Christie and Hanlon, as above.

## Chapter 15

(1) In Mozambique children repeat grades if they do not pass end of year tests. Daniel has made good progress but has not moved up a grade every year.

## Chapter 17

(1) See Appendix for Pastor Rego's account of his life.

## Chapter 18

(1) Go to www.wmpress.org for more information on World Missionary Press and its work around the world.

## Chapter 19

(1) Go to www.making-disciples.net for more information on Yanit and Reuven Ross's discipleship ministry.

## Chapter 21

(1) Go to www.foundationsforfarming.org for a fuller explanation of the basis of this farming.

(2) www.mullers.org/global

*This delightful design, used throughout the book, was adapted from a childhood sketch by Tanneken and expresses so well the spirit of this book.*

To connect with TCF Mercy
you may visit http://tcfmercy.org

Made in the USA
Monee, IL
20 July 2020